THE

UNEXPECTED

REBELLION

THE
UNEXPECTED
REBELLION

Ethnic Activism in Contemporary France

William R. Beer

New York University Press. New York *and* London

Library of Congress Cataloging in Publication Data
Beer, William R   1943-
   The unexpected rebellion.

   Bibliography: p.
   Includes index.
   1. Regionalism—France.   2. Ethnology—France.
I. Title.
JN2610.R4B43   323.1'44   79-3515
ISBN 0-8147-1029-8

Manufactured in the United States of America

To my father

Preface

During the summer of 1972, while I was living in a village of Anjou and completing the research for my doctoral dissertation on social change in rural France, two young Breton nationalists happened to visit me. They gave me my first introduction to history from the point of view of the peoples who had been absorbed during the formation of the French nation. It was a perspective quite different from the one I had learned as an undergraduate, which had portrayed the expansion of the French state as logical and natural. Their perception was one of a foreign power subjugating an independent Celtic nation.

Most memorable was their view of Bretons as living both in their homeland and in a diaspora, with exiles in Paris, among the French military and colonial administrations, and even in North America. "Why," one of them said to me, "one of your greatest American writers was a Breton!" I was ashamed when I could not identify him, but when they named Jack Kerouac, I was less embarrassed. I had always thought of Kerouac as of French Canadian ancestry, but more important to them was his descent from Breton nobility. I realized that ethnic sentiment in France was a powerful prism that refracted far differently from any I had seen before.

As a Fulbright Junior Lecturer in Strasbourg in 1974–75, I attended a colloquium on Regions and Regionalism in France from the Eighteenth Century to the Present, and was lucky to meet its organizer, Professor Christian Gras of the Institut d'Histoire Economique et Sociale. Professor Gras and I began a collaboration that continues to this day, and he graciously made available to me the facilities of his Institute. During that year I carried out a survey of the leaders of ethnic activist groups that is the basis for part of this book. Without the help of Professor Grass, the survey would not have been completed and this book not written. I am deeply grateful for his generosity.

I would like to express my gratitude to the Council for International Exchange of Scholars, which administered the Fulbright Lectureship during which I carried out much of the research for this book. The Research Foundation of the City University of New York provided additional support. I would also like to thank Professor Marilyn Gittell of Brooklyn College for her assistance.

In preparing this book, I wrote many papers that reported parts of my research, and tested the validity of my analyses with criticism and comment by professional audiences. I would like to thank Professor Orville Menard of the University of Nebraska at Omaha for giving me the opportunity on two occasions to present my work at the University of Nebraska's European Studies Conference. Professor Bernard Brown was also kind enough to allow me to present a report on my research to the City University of New York Colloquium on European Studies, and I am grateful for his subsequent invitation to participate in the Colloquium. Professor Nicholas Wahl invited me to present a paper at Princeton University, where I learned much from the comment and criticism I received. I have also profited greatly from conferences he organized at the Institute of French Studies of New York University. Professor Werner Cahnman of the Seminar on Cultural Pluralism at Columbia University, Professor George Romoser of the Conference Group on German Politics and Society, Professor Allan Schwartzbaum of Viginia

Commonwealth University, and Professor Martin Heisler of the International Studies Association also gave me the opportunity to discuss my findings with my colleagues, and I am grateful to them.

Professor Milton Esman of the Cornell University Center for International Studies gave me the patience and support I needed when I was first writing on the subject of ethnic activism. In 1975, he invited me to the Conference on Ethnic Pluralism and Conflict in Western Europe and Canada, to give a paper that was subsequently published. I owe him a great deal for starting me on the course that led to this book. Professor Ray Hall of Dartmouth College also deserves my thanks for having organized the Conference on Ethnic Separatism in 1978, which was as delightful as it was intellectually rewarding, and for editing a volume in which my paper is included.

Madame G. Tuma of the Service de Presse of the French Consulate in New York deserves my special thanks. During my many visits to the Service's library she was always kind and helpful, taking an interest in my research and providing information where it was not always easy to find. Her diligence and charm made my research there a real pleasure.

Finally, although he had no direct connection to this study, I must acknowledge my debt to Professor Laurence Wylie of Harvard University. During a seminar on French civilization while I was at Harvard, and during a period of fieldwork in western France that he made possible, Professor Wylie made French culture alive, exciting, and understandable to me. His informality, his intimate knowledge of the people, his refusal to be confined by orthodox disciplines inspired in me a passion for the study of France that will never wane.

Contents

Contents

Tables and Illustrations

Introduction

It is well known that ethnic conflict threatens the unity of new nations that have emerged since World War II. Since 1960, ethnic militancy has made an unexpected reappearance in more modern societies as well. The legitimacy of relatively long-established states has recently been sharply questioned, in Canada by the Québecois, in Britain by the Scots and Welsh, in Spain by Basques and Catalans, in Belgium by both Flemings and Walloons, and in Switzerland by the French of the Jura. There are also ethnic movements in seven regions of France, among Alsatians, Flemings, Bretons, Basques, Catalans, Occitans, and Corsicans.[1]

To seek to understand ethnic activism is to examine the origins of a force that is not only threatening new nations but calling into question even those which have existed for centuries. This book is an exploration of ethnic activism in one of the oldest nation-states. France has long seemed a paragon of national unity, possessing a national language and a centralized administration whose beginnings date back to the fourteenth century. That ethnic regionalist, federalist, autonomist, and separatist groups have appeared in great

numbers there, is testimony that powerful and long-dormant forces
are at work again. What are the historic antecedents of these movements? Why have they appeared now? Who are their leaders? How
are these observations instructive about ethnic activism elsewhere?

The definition of ethnicity used here is based on that of Francis:

> "Ethnicity" refers to the fact that (1) a relatively large number
> of people are socially defined as belonging together because of
> a belief in their being descended from common ancestors; that
> (2) because of this belief, they have a sense of identity and
> share sentiments of solidarity. (Francis, 1976: 382)

This conception is consistent with others that take self-definition as
a basic characteristic of ethnicity, such as Enloe (1973: 16), Patterson (1975: 309), and DeVos (1975: 16-17). The sentiments of solidarity based on belief in common descent are also consistent with
the boundary-maintaining properties of ethnicity considered funda-
mental by Barth (1969: 15), and its interest-group functions pointed
out by Glazer and Moynihan (1975: 7). The bases of this sense of
solidarity and identity consist of common cultural characteristics
(Van den Berghe, 1970: 10), and of these the most important is
often language. Tumin (1964: 243) and Parsons (1975: 53-83), for
instance, agree that language is a central aspect of ethnicity.[2]

The phrase "ethnic activism" is used for brevity and inclusive-
ness. Ethnic regionalism seeks redistribution of valued resources
within the framework of the state, whereas ethnic nationalism
seeks a new political entity (Jacob, 1978; Reece, 1977). The latter
can, in turn, be subdivided into other types. Autonomism charac-
terizes movements that seek special status for their region, though
not necessarily separate status. Separatism is a type of nationalism
that seeks the most radical disassociation, in the form of a separate
state. Federalism is a different sort of ethnic activism, seeking autonomy in a federal state, which for France would require total
rearrangement of the political superstructure. Besides these overtly
political types of ethnic activism, there are folklore, literary, and
linguistic organizations. All these types of activity are present in

France today, and are referred to collectively as ethnic activism.[3] Table I.2 (below) shows a breakdown of these types of ethnic activist organizations.

Using language as a basis referent characteristic, France has seven ethnic regions: Alsace, French Flanders, Brittany, the French Basque Country, French Catalonia, Occitania, and Corsica. Both the geographic and demographic boundaries of each ethnic region are far from precise (see Figure I.1)

Alsace, referred to by its Germanic name *Elsass* by activists, includes the departments of Haut-Rhin and Bas-Rhin, where most of the population of one and a half million speak a Germanic dialect in addition to French. The region is bounded on the west by the Vosges mountains, and on the east by the Rhine. To the north is the German Saarland, and to the south, Switzerland. The river has historically been less of a barrier to invaders than have the mountains, keeping Alsace under the cultural influence of peoples to the east, as well as a prize long coveted by their leaders. The Alsatians are an anomaly both to Germans and to other Frenchmen, the former regarding them as Frenchifield Germans, and the latter as Germanized Frenchmen. They are thus a marginal people in the classic sense, but this condition has not had the dire effects that might be expected. Alsatian culture is a synthesis of the Germanic and the French, with which the Alsatians themselves are at ease.

Alsace has often been paired with an area west of the Vosges that includes parts of the departments of Vosges, Moselle, and Meurtheet-Moselle, where a Germanic dialect is still spoken by some elements in the population. This region is known as Lorraine, which has also been attached to and detached from Germany periodically. It is not considered in this study, however. Not only have French language and culture made far greater inroads there, but to date no signs of ethnic activism have appeared. Many Alsatian activists are fond of referring to the region as Alsace-Lorraine (Elsass-Lothringen), but the fact is that ethnic activism is confined to Alsace proper.

Language difference is the major aspect of ethnicity in Alsace, as it is in France's other ethnic regions. Only a few elderly people

Figure I.1. Ethnic Regions of France and their Departments.

speak no French at all, and only people from the interior speak French exclusively. Alsatian identity is thus shared by an essentially bilingual population (Hoffet, 1951: 59; Legris, 1964). In general, the dialect is spoken at home and among friends, and French is the language of business.

French Flanders is a linguistic and ethnic spillover from the Flemish-speaking areas in Belgium. It includes the northern part of the department of Nord, and a northwestern part of the department of Pas-de-Calais known as Westhoek. "The region," says a description by a French Fleming, "is not known for being attractive from the point of view of tourism, industry or culture" (Vandewalle, 1976: 251). Its principal cities are Lille and Dunkerque, but Flemish influence is notable only in the latter. There are no clear geographic demarcations between French and Flemish-speaking areas in this flat farmland. Flemish cultural and linguistic influences, in any case, are much weaker here than with Germanic culture in Alsace. The two departments have about 4 million inhabitants, of whom about 100,000 to 200,000 speak Flemish, depending on the source consulted (Fougeyrollas, 1968; Uss'm Follik, 1974). In French Flanders, too, Flemish ethnicity is bilingual.

Brittany (*Breizh*, in the Breton language) is a peninsula that reaches westward toward the Celtic lands of Britain. It is not difficult to identify geographically, because it includes the departments of Ille-et-Vilaine, Morbihan, Finistère, and Côtes-du-Nord. Some militants claim that Nantes is a part of Brittany, because Nantes was a Breton city before 1532, but it is not considered as such in the present study. Brittany is a region distinct from the rest of western France, as a celebrated Breton writer once described it. When leaving Normandy and entering Brittany, wrote Renan, "A cold wind arises full of a vague sadness, and carries the soul to other thoughts; the treetops are bare and twisted; the heath with its monotony of tint stretches away into the distance; at every step the granite protrudes from a soil too scanty to cover it; a sea that is almost always somber girdles the horizon with eternal moaning" (Renan, 1910: 143).

The ethnic and linguistic borders of Brittany are considerably cloudier, however. The Breton language is Celtic, akin to Welsh, Manx, Cornish, and the Scottish and Irish varieties of Gaelic. Other cultural artifacts are shared among these Celtic lands also, such as the bagpipe. Although at one time Breton was spoken as far east as Rennes, it is not spoken today west of St. Brieuc and Vannes. Breton identity, however, is claimed not only by people who speak Breton but also by those who speak a Breton dialect of French called Gallo, as well as by some who speak pure French but have Breton names or ancestry. In the western part of the peninsula are about 500,000 people who speak Gaelic Breton (Le Gris, 1964). But in the eastern part of the province the Gallo dialects are spoken, which, even though they are Romance rather than Gaelic, are considered Breton. An indeterminate number of people in these departments consider themselves Breton simply because this is where they live; other French speakers who have emigrated also consider themselves Breton because of where they came from.

Florus, a Roman historian, commented on the ancient Basques, "Nearly all of Spain was pacified except that part of the Pyrenees where the nearby Ocean battered the crags. There resisted two of the most valiant of all nations, the Cantabrians and Asturians [the Basques] who were not affected by the conquest . . ." (Sacx, 1968: 18). The major part of Euzkadi, the Basque homeland, is in Spain, but part of it extends north into France. The French Basques are concentrated in the department of Pyrénées-Atlantiques in the areas known as Soule, Labourde, and Basse-Navarre. The Spanish Basque region is heavily industrialized, but the French Basque Country, outside the coastal city of Bayonne, is substantially rural and pastoral. The Basques are an ancient people, and their language is unrelated to any other now in existence. It has been suggested that they are the original stone-age inhabitants of the area, because the word for "stone" in Basque appears in most words referring to hand tools. Of the 535,000 people in the department of Pyrénées-Atlantiques, about 80,000 speak Basque (LeGris, 1964). But in the French Basque Country are also an indeterminate number of French speakers who consider themselves Basque because of their residence, origin, or family names. The Basques, Spanish and

French, have traditionally been devout Catholics, so that relations between them and the French authorities have been strained at those times when government policy was anticlerical. There has always been strong transfrontier solidarity among Basques. The first rebellion by them against the French occurred in 630. "The Basques, having formed a great army under the command of their duke Amandus, ravaged the land under the King's authority. Their forces . . . were also reinforced with the help of the Basques of Spain, their neighbors . . ." (Sacx, 1968: 24). Such reinforcement continues to this day.

Greater Catalonia, Catalunya, is made up of several geographic components. The largest is Spanish Catalonia, which includes the *principat* around Barcelona, Valencia, and the Balearic Islands. It also includes the Principality of Andorra, in the Pyrenees, where it is the official language. It is spoken in a city in Sardinia, Alguero. Finally, French Catalonia is formed by the area known as Róussillon, in the department of Pyrénées-Orientales. French Catalans make up some 200,000 of the 299,000 people in the department (LeGris, 1964; Héraud, 1966).

The island of Corsica, recently divided into the departments of Haute-Corse and Corse-du-Sud, is the home of another ethnic group who are as marginal as the Alsatians. As one traveler describes it, "Corsica is France, but it is not French. It is a mountain range moored like a great ship with a cargo of crags a hundred miles off the Riviera. In its three climates it combines the high Alps, the ruggedness of North Africa and the choicest landscapes of Italy, but most dramatic are the peaks which are never out of view and show in the upheaval of rock a culture that is violent and heroic" (Theroux, 1978: 90). The Corsican dialect is often thought of as a remote dialect of Italian but it is directly descended from Latin. Most of the 200,000 inhabitants of the island speak the dialect as well as French. As in Alsace, use of the dialect is reserved for familiar conversations, but French is used in public. And like Alsace, Corsica has contributed some of France's most illustrious military heroes, most notable of whom was Napoleon Bonaparte.

Occitania has been left till last, because it poses many problems of definition. In general, it refers to the areas of France where the southern "oc" dialects, as opposed to the northern "oïl" dialects, were spoken before the national consolidation of France. By the broadest definition, Occitania includes all of southern France (La-font, 1971: 12). Thus defined, Occitania is little more than a word, because it includes such industrial areas as Marseille, Toulouse, and Bordeaux, along with poverty-stricken areas such as Ardèche and Cantal, not to speak of the fabulously wealthy Côte d'Azur. It is also culturally heterogeneous, because it includes the Italian-influenced area of Piedmont, along with the Spanish- and Catalan-influenced parts of south and south-central France. Others consider Occitania in the more restricted sense of the latter, the mountainous areas of southern France adjoining Spain and Catalonia (e.g., Marti, 1975: 23). It includes regions where distinct dialects of Occitan are spoken, the principal ones being Gascon, Langedocien, Provençal, and Nord-Occitan. But even though these varieties of Occitan are spoken in different areas, we have little clear information about the numbers who speak them and the social groups they belong to. Thus, there is a geographic approximation of the areas where some dialects are spoken, but the depth and nature of these linguistic groups are far from clear. Occitan militants like to claim the widest possible membership, yet the government compiles no figures at all. Inconvenient though it may be, we must recognize that Occitania exists, but that its precise demographic and social dimensions are at present unknown. In this essay, it is considered to include the department of Haute-Vienne, Creuse, Corrèze, Allier, Puy-de-Dôme, Cantal, Haute-Loire, Lot, Aveyron, Tarn-et-Caronne, Tarn, Haute-Garonne, Gers, Hautes-Pyrénées, Ariège, Dordogne, Lot-et-Garonne, Lozère, Gard, Hérault, Aude, Drôme, Ardèche, Hautes-Alpes, Vaucluse, and Alpes-de-Haute-Provence. Thus, Occitania is considered in its larger dimension, but the coastal area of Bordeaux, the area around Marseille, and the Côte d'Azur have been left out.

In all these regions, language is used as the defining characteristic of ethnicity, both because it is the repository of culture and because of the importance placed on well-spoken French by the

French themselves. It is not simply the existence of a distinct dialect or language that demarcates these ethnic groups from other Frenchmen. Some dialects such as Alsatian, Occitan, and Corsican leave their mark in the form of accented French. An Alsatian accent, for instance, is as glaring a marker of ethnic difference as the Alsatian dialect itself. It is difficult to overstate the importance of perfectly pronounced French in France, and much ridicule is incurred by minorities whose accents are different.

Though these are all ethnic regions in the sense that they contain people who claim an ethnic identity distinct from that of being French, they are very different from one another. They vary widely in their degrees of economic underdevelopment and the speed at which this underdevelopment is being erased. Alsace and Flanders have long been among the most industrialized areas in France, while Brittany, Occitania and Corsica have been notorious for their rurality and poverty. Brittany is rapidly industrializing, while Occitania's development has been less rapid. The history of ethnic activism in each area is also very different, and the contemporary strength and number of ethnic activist groups is relatively great in Brittany and Corsica, while in Flanders and Alsace relatively small.

These seven are the ethnic regions studied in this book, but they are not the only areas in which movements have appeared claiming some regional distinctiveness. The Young Normandy Movement (Mouvement de Jeunesse de la Normandie) has appeared in Normandy, and a group called Eklitra has been formed in Picardy. In Savoy, there are the Movement for a Savoy Region (Mouvement pour une Region-Savoie) and the Savoyard Regionalist Alliance (Rassemblement Regionaliste Savoyard); more militant are Free Savoy (Savoie Libre) and Legitimate Savoy (Savoie Legitime). But neither Normandy nor Picardy can be thought of as ethnic regions, because although there are dialects spoken in the areas, they are dialects of French. The same is more or less true of French Savoy. These can be considered as regionalist movements, but not ethnic activist movements, and thus are not considered.

The sociological study of a social movement requires two types of investigation, the specific origins of the movement and the gen-

eral processes at work in it. The first are of a historical nature and
the second are in the form of theoretically derived propositions and
hypotheses that can be tested in all similar circumstances. Chapter
I below presents the historic background of ethnic activism in
France, and Chapter II explains why its contemporary manifesta-
tion is a problem for social science. Then follow two chapters
examining the two basic components of the movement, the underlying conditions that give rise to it, and the characteristics of the
leadership. Both of these treatments are in the form of testing hypotheses derived from social theory, because the aim is to understand ethnic activism in contexts other than that of contemporary
France. The final chapter is an attempt at synthesis of the historical, theoretical, and empirical material into an assessment of the
nature of ethnic activism in contemporary France and elsewhere,
and what is likely to become of it.

FOREWORD

If modern democratic theory is correct then ethnic activism is one of the recent developments that most threaten western government—its stability, effectiveness and legitimacy. This is because ethnic activists, along with members of so-called "single issue" pressure groups such as environmentalists, refuse to play by the rules of the pluralist democratic game. They resist efforts to federate or "aggregate" them into broad coalitions of interests which lend stability, effectiveness and legitimacy to governments and their policies. This is because their very nature requires them to reject the common denominator offered by the federating political parties or party coalitions for this nature affirms the transcendent interest of ethnic survival or revival. Neither class solidarity nor economic interest nor the appeal of charismatic authority nor even religion can serve as the common denominator to attract the ethnic activist toward permanent cooperation with those outside his group.

With the political organization of ethnic and "single-issue" activists, it is argued, stable governing majorities become difficult to

maintain and governmental performance declines. Political parties
lose their functions as federators of interests and become empty
shells, circulating power among an increasingly isolated elite. Popular confidence in democratic government recedes and a crisis of
democracy is declared. Whether or not ethnic activism is a major
cause of such a crisis depends, to be sure, on both the acceptance of
such theories of pluralist democracy and the importance of the
ethnic phenomenon. But that ethnicity in western politics is a
problem that has taken on new dimensions in recent years is surely
beyond question.

France's experience with ethnic activism is especially interesting
for cultural as well as political reasons. The monism of French
culture and the centralization of French politics would appear to
allow scant legitimacy and little hope for the ethnic activists. Yet,
as William Beer has shown in the pages to follow, France has a long
history of ethnic politics and one that has demonstrated the activists' ability to adapt to changing conditions. When centralizing
efforts came from the left the activists mobilized support by em-
ploying conservative and anti-democratic themes. When centralization was pursued by the right it was radicalism and grass-roots
democracy that served as the vehicle of ethnic activist recruitment.
But in both cases the strictly political themes were subordinated to
the transcendent value of ethnic solidarity, an interest transcendent
over all others including, often, the national interest. Thus ethnic
politics in France has been considered subversive of one of the
nation's oldest civic values—the reality of a "public good," defined
for the nation as a whole by central political institutions and pursued by a centralized state machine.

Early in the century anti-parliamentary monarchists and more
recently revolutionary socialists have joined ethnic activists in the
rejection of the notion of a "public good" legitimately defined by
the political majority of the moment. Only the ethnic activists have
always rejected *any* notion of a "French" public good that could
transcend class, region and ideology. For the activist ethnic loyalty
has the force of class, region and ideology all combined: it is a
loyalty to a true nation within an artificial nation. But for tradi-

tional French culture and politics, born in the context of the nation whose "artificiality" is a source of historic pride, there can be no nation within *the* nation. It was to end such a situation that Kings and revolutions forged the "artificial" French nation, as young Frenchmen continue to be taught. And the uniqueness of French culture and politics—and hence French national identity—has been related to the centralization and the resultant monism of French education, administration, economy, law and literary and linguistic institutions, all imposed upon more "natural" institutions by the center.

This relationship between centralization, nationhood and sense of collective identity continues to be powerful and self-reinforcing. Some years ago when France was debating a modest regionalization reform, I attended the final parliamentary discussion of the government bill. During an interval I asked one of the main opponents why he was so adamant in light of the bill's timid provisions for local self-rule. "Because," he said, "the genius of France lies in centralized institutions: to dilute them ever so slightly is to take a major step toward abandoning what makes us seem different." "Different" from the English, the Germans and the Americans was, of course, what my conservative Jacobin friend had in mind. That Frenchmen, such as the ethnic activists, would want to insist on what made them different from each other was conceivable for him but totally subversive and reckless. I doubt whether a more left-wing Jacobin would have substantially different feelings on the subject. On the basis of past experience the left in power quickly loses much of its decentralizing fervor. If ethnic activism continues to grow it will offer a challenge to any government because it strikes at the heart of both the reigning value system and established political procedures accepted by both left and right.

What are the causes of the current revival of ethnic activism and its challenge to traditional French democracy and culture? There are curious ironies in the explanations offered by Professor Beer in this book. He suggests that French participation in the regional and international economic systems has undermined the credibility of the nation as a viable unit. An emerging European economy, it has been argued, gives new potential to the sub-national unit of the region. It is true that supporters of a supra-national European economic integration have long been proponents of regionalization and decentralization. Following the ancient diplomatic dictum, "the enemy of your enemy is your friend," they view whatever saps the nation state as encouraging supra-national development. The irony here is that today's supra-nationalists are the heirs of a nineteenth century rationalism that saw the interdependence of nations as leading to a decline of nationalisms as well as ethnic patriotisms. Yet today's European interdependence is seen as encouraging ethnic activism within the old national communities, quite a counter-historical development for some observers.

A more "rational," if unintended, encouragement to ethnicity in politics, according to Beer, has come from various governments' efforts at decentralizing administrative procedures, if not actual decision making. From the creation of the Committes for Regional Economic Development (CODER) to the activities of the Regional Planning Agency (DATAR), Jacobin Gaullism has appeared to legitimize the idea of local responsibility for the social and economic development of the region. What is more natural, then, than that this development should have a cultural and linguistic dimension in those areas where a regional ethnic culture has persisted? Here the irony resides in the central government's expectations of greater efficiency coming from administrative decentralization while for the activists these reforms represent steps toward regional autonomy—which Paris did not think of for a monent. Yet I doubt that such timid progress toward limited decentralization will continue to encourage the activists in the future. Opinion polls have not shown much support for real decentralization and while the Socialist Party's program offers lip service to regional government, the bulk of its reforms requires rather massive centralized controls rather than a Girondist devolution of power. The long struggle for democracy in France has, in fact, made Jacobins of everyone: for the left centralization is the condition for equality; for the right it has become the last bulwark against upheaval.

The third major cause of ethnic activism, in Professor Beer's view, is the example provided by world-wide decolonization and the well publicized efforts of national liberation movements in the Third World. Here, too, there is irony in the French case. For after having been one of the most tragically active opponents of national self-determination in Indochina and Algeria, France under de Gaulle became the west's main champion of subject "nations"— from de Gaulle's critique of. American intervention in South East Asia to his cry of "Vive le Québec Libre" in Montreal. Surely for an old Jacobin such as the General the prospect of his words giving comfort to Breton and Basque nationalists would have been painful to say the least. But it must be said that during his last year in power de Gaulle did seem to be moving toward a revision of his views on the virtues of centralization. His championship of national revivals in the Third World and Quebec may have had something to do with his sudden espousal of regionalization in 1968-69—a shift that antedated, it should be noted, the events of May 1968.

But even more important in changing his mind was an indirect result of a central Gaullist policy: the rapid, forced-draft industrialization launched in the mid-1960's. For a shrewd realist such as de Gaulle it must have become obvious that the remarkable rise of living standards throughout much of France would create rising expectations in more marginal areas, especially those marginal both economically *and* ethnically, such as Brittany. This was a time, it should be remembered, when similar contrasts between peripheral poverty and central prosperity were generating discussion of devolution of power in Great Britain and Italy. A measure of regional self-government may well have appeared to de Gaulle as a small price for maintaining domestic calm at a time when he had important goals to achieve on the international scene.

After de Gaulle France's industrialization and urbanization continued at the same pace. The social strains that resulted are shown by Professor Beer to have helped produce the leadership of contemporary ethnic activism. The rootless local intellectuals, searching for a simpler,more stable and more satisfying life in a world beset by inflation and changing values, have turned to ethnic revival and defense as a refuge. For the farmers, artisans and small-town professionals who are disoriented by rapid social change this leadership has emerged at the right time. Ethnic activism, of course, serves to bring national attention to their economic grievances but, as Beer suggests, it also helps them to resolve problems of individual identity in a national context that appears increasingly threatening to traditional outlooks on the most essential matters—family, work, leisure, etc. France was long a country in which, more than elsewhere, the individual sense of identity was protected by a strong traditional cultural fabric, relatively slow economic growth and limited social mobility. Rapid industrialization, urban sprawl and growing economic and, indeed, cultural dependence upon regional and overseas hinterlands has changed all this.

It remains to be seen whether or not ethnic activism will make a positive contribution to France's adaptation to post-industrial conditions. It could do this by becoming primarily a force in favor of regional government rather than an archaic movement in favor of cultural autonomy and as such a minor phenomenon of pressure group politics. If ethnic activism contributes to genuine regionalization in France it will have served a practical purpose and helped to ease the strains of rapid social change. Yet the great majority of Frenchmen do not live in areas where a truly regional identity is available. For them the highest loyalty remains old Jacobin nationhood, damaged a bit by the forces described below, but still the main source of self-definition for the French today. Possibly in the distant future there will arise a European identity to replace the French one born of Kings and revolutions. Ethnic activism may then be viewed by historians as having contributed to this evolution in some small way. For the time being, however, it remains one of a number of phenomena which raise questions about the relevance of pluralist democratic theory and the effectiveness of parliamentary government in the traditional national setting.

Nicholas Wahl

CHAPTER ONE

The History of Ethnic Activism
in France

The strength of ethnic activism in France today is greater than in any previous period. Each of the seven ethnic regions has some militancy, even if it is limited to cultural preservation, and in some areas militancy has gone beyond even electoral politics into the realm of terrorism. But these contemporary manifestations are not without precedent. In tracing their antecedents, as well as the factors leading up to the recent renaissance, the specifically French causes of ethnic activism will be revealed. Before looking at each region's history of ethnic activism, let us first consider how these peoples came to be a part of France at all.

In French schoolbooks, the "hexagonal" dimensions of the nation are depicted as following some natural or divine will that led France to have the borders she has now. Geographically speaking, France is enclosed by the natural borders of mountains and oceans on the southeast, south, west, and north, but not on the east or northeast. In the latter two dwell two of her ethnic minorities, Alsatians and Flemings, whose membership in the nation is more the result of state policy than of nature. If mountains are to be

1

taken as a natural border, then France should stop at the Vosges, and Alsace should be part of Germany. As for Flanders, there simply is no natural boundary that might explain Flemings' French citizenship. Even where there are natural boundaries, ethnic groups span all of them: Bretons have ethnic cousins across the Channel in Britain and Ireland, Basques and Catalans across the Pyrenees in Spain. Corsica is no more naturally a part of France than Sardinia, and the Corsican dialect has much more in common with Italian than with French.

In spite of myths about national unity, France was created by the systematic conquest and annexation of territory and peoples by the French-speaking agents of the Crown, which as late as the eleventh century held sway only in the restricted area around Paris known as the Ile de France. The essential process underlying French history from Hugh Capet (987-996) to Louis XIV (1643-1715) was the steady addition of territory and centralization of administration by the king. Regardless of the modernization and rationalization that the formation of the national state may have entailed, it required the invasion and suppression of peoples, who, in language and customs, had little in common with the French.[1] The modern manifestations of ethnic activism are, according to some interpretations, the continuation of resistance on the part of subject peoples. Whether this interpretation is accepted or not, contemporary ethnic activism cannot be understood without an explanation of its historical genesis.

If the initial annexation of each territory is the starting point in this history, the Revolution constitutes its turning point. In spite of the frequently ruthless subjection to royal power, under the old regime each territory retained some special characteristics, and in some cases formal autonomy. But Napoleon abolished the old provinces and substituted for them departments of a more or less standard size. Each department was subsequently under the administration of a prefect, who was appointed in Paris. Parallel to and ultimately more powerful than elected officials was a bureaucracy totally centralized in the capital. Rational though the decision was, the departments and the rule of the prefects fragmented the old ethnic territories and subjected them to the uniform rule of Paris. This geographic revolution was consistent with the Jacobin policy of equating Frenchness with the Revolution. In such a system there was no place for ethnic particularisms. A revolutionary minister declared:

> We have revolutionized the government, customs and thought; let us also revolutionize language. Federalism and superstition speak Bas-Breton, emigration and hatred of the Republic speak German; counterrevolution speaks Italian; fanaticism speaks Basque. . . . (Sérant, 1965: 30-31)

Accordingly, in November 1793, a decree was issued that all children had to be taught to read, speak, and write in French.

For many years after, ethnic activism was therefore largely expressed as opposition to the Revolution. The conservatism of these movements continued until the morrow of World War II. There are three general periods, then, in which we can treat the history of each region's relationship to France: the pre-Revolutionary, the period between the Revolution and the Liberation in 1945, and the postwar revival. The factors leading to the latter will be examined in detail, and the chapter will finish with a sketch of developments in each region from 1964 to 1979.

1. THE ETHNIC REGIONS UP TO THE REVOLUTION

The first of France's ethnic areas to be conquered was what is today known as Occitania. Although this name was long in use as a linguistic designation, it has come to refer to a geographic and ethnic entity only since World War II. It is composed of distinct regions, the principal ones being Gascony, Guienne, Aquitaine, Provence, and Languedoc. Each of these included different versions of speech that can generally be characterized as "langue d'oc," opposed to the "langue d'oïl" of the North of France. "Oc" and "oïl" are two ways of saying "yes," which was used as an indication of the different evolution of vulgate Latin in the two parts of France. The latter has come to be spelled "oui," and the fact that it is standard French demonstrates the political and cultural preeminence of the North.

Although they had language similarities, the provinces of the South had cultural elements in common as well. It was in the langue d'oc that the cultural renaissance of the twelfth century was expressed, and the exquisite flowering of the troubadours and the *chansons de geste* were expressions of Occitan culture. Besides linguistic and cultural similarities, the duchies of the South also came to share the pervasive influence of a heretical and austere version of Christianity known as Catharism.

The extirpation of this heresy was the pretense by which the French crown joined the Albigensian Crusade, whose official purpose was to restore the authority of Innocent III, but which led to extension of the king's power to the Mediterranean. Simon de Montfort was the leader of this expedition, and the horrors he perpetrated at Muret in 1213 and elsewhere led to total suppression of the heresy, of resistance to the French, and of the brilliant Provençal culture. By 1226 the Crusade was over and the greater part of Occitania was French. The acquisition of Gascony, Guienne, and Aquitaine was not complete until after English control over these duchies was decisively erased in the Hundred Years' War (1338-1453). In general, then, the conquest of Occitania by the French was the product of some two-hundred years of warfare.

The suppression of Occitan culture was so successful that there was little subsequent expression of ethnic opposition until the Revolution. However, the strength of Protestantism in the South during the Wars of Religion can be partially explained by the residual resentment against the Catholic monarchy. The revolt of the Camisards was based in Occitan territory, and there were certainly ethnic overtones in the ferociousness of its suppression. From 1160 until the Revolution a systematic campaign was directed against the language of the South, which was derided as *patois*, from the dialect of Poitiers.[2]

The pre-Revolutionary history of Occitania helps to explain one of the most important episodes in the Revolution: the struggle between the Girondins and the Mountain. The former were originally deputies from the Occitan department of Gironde, and their ideology was a form of federalism. Their interest in diminishing Parisian authority was at least partially inspired by the opposition to Jacobin centralism, with its hostility to ethnic minorities. The suppression of the Gironde by the Mountain in 1793 was as much a victory of centralism over federalism as one of the far left over more moderate voices (see Aulard, 1968: 140).

Although later subordinated to France, Brittany was itself formed by conquest and colonization of the peninsula by Celtic tribes from Britain between the fifth and seventh centuries. The original Gallic inhabitants of the area were subjugated by people who came to be thought of as Bretons. Although common cultural characteristics remain between the subsequent Breton culture and that of the original inhabitants, Brittany is certainly the result of Celtic invasion and colonization (McDonald, 1978: 9).

Until 1532, Brittany was an autonomous entity, but because of Norman, English, Angevin, and French royal pressures, had never again achieved the glory of King Nominoë when he defeated Charles the Bald at Bain-sur-Ost in 845. During the Hundred Years' War, the Breton duchy was first on one side and then the other. The crucial figure in the eventual alliance of Brittany with France in this conflict was Bertrand Du Guesclin, whom French history books depict as a hero and Breton nationalists as a traitor. There followed a complicated succession, which led to formal annexation of Brittany. After the French victory of St-Aubin-du-Cormier in 1488, Duke François of Brittany renounced the sovereign rights of the duchy and agreed not to marry his daughter without the consent of the French king. His daughter was obliged to marry King Louis IX; this marriage of persons and politics was sealed by the Treaty of 1532.

The legality of the treaty is still questioned by some activists, but whatever the legitimacy of the process whereby it came to be established, the terms of the treaty clearly safeguarded Brittany's autonomy. They included preservation of the Breton Assembly and prohibition against taxation of Bretons without their consent

(Sérant, 1971: 29). From then until the Revolution, however, the terms of the Act of Union were only partially observed, and there were repeated Breton revolts against French authority. The imposition of heavy taxes, in violation of the treaty, led to a peasant revolt, the Bonnets Rouges, in 1675, whose suppression was accompanied by many atrocities. Continuing resistance to taxation led sixty Breton noblemen to send a petition to the king in 1718 declaring their loyalty to him, but citing the terms of the treaty. Twenty of them were executed in royal retaliation. The strife between the Breton Estates and the crown over the right of taxation continued throughout the eighteenth century.

Breton resistance to the centralizing efforts of the Revolution can be understood by reflecting on the previous resistance to absolutism. The Breton parliament was abolished in 1790, and beginning in 1793 a counterrevolutionary movement erupted in western France, Breton and non-Breton alike. It centered at first in the Vendée, which gave its name to the whole rebellion. Though ferociously suppressed by the government, anti-Republican guerrilla activity, known as *chouannerie,* persisted in Brittany. Observers spoke of long lines of trees bending under the weight of corpses hanging from their limbs, and mass drownings of civilians were organized in Nantes. Although much of the counterrevolution can be explained by differential rates of urbanization in these areas (see, e.g., Tilly, 1964), it had an ethnic component in Brittany.[3] Later Breton expressions of counterrevolution included an attempt in 1794 to coordinate with a British expeditionary force; an attempted assassination of Napoleon by the Breton nationalist Prigent in 1800; a mutiny against Napoleon led by General Cadoudal in 1804; and a "little *chouannerie,*" led by De Grisolles, during the Hundred Days in 1814. Finally, Caro, a Breton organizer of the legitimist plot of 1832, was hanged after this was defeated.

One of the first and most celebrated contacts between French and Basques was when Charlemagne's rear guard was attacked at Roncesvalles and Roland made his heroic stand. The attackers were Basques, though they are not so identified in the *Chanson de Roland.* Most Basques live in Spain, but there has always been a province of Euzkadi (the Basque name for the Basque nation) north of the Pyrénées as well, composed of the French territories of Soule, Labourde, and Mauléon. Euzkadi was once united under the Navarrese Sancho the Great (999-1035), but this unity was short-lived, caught as it was between the powerful and expanding monarchies to the North and South.

In 1589, Henry of Navarre became Henry IV of France, and the Basques north of the Pyrenees were from then on part of the French realm. In theory, the Basques were protected by charters of autonomy—called *fueros* in Spanish and *fors* in French—which preserved their legal independence from taxation until the nineteenth century (Greenwood, 1975). In 1620, Louis XIII even proclaimed a formal "Edict of Union," which promised some autonomy, but there were repeated abuses and rebellions until the end of the old regime. The Revolution, for its own reasons, attempted to suppress Basque autonomy. The rebellion against abolition of the fors and the Civil Constitution of the Clergy was treated harshly. Four thousand suspect people were deported to Gascony, of whom between 1,600 and 2,000 perished (Galloy, 1966: 55).

Until the victory of De Montfort at Muret, Catalonia and Occitania formed a culturally similar grouping of duchies. The counts of Barcelona had ruled not only a large part of northeastern Spain, but the Balearic Islands and the territories of Roussillon and Cerdagne as well. With the French expansion southward, Catalan political power north of the Pyrenees waned. After the Treaty of Corbeil in 1258, French Catalonia remained a part of Catalonia, but the focus of Barcelona's attention shifted to the Iberian peninsula. In the fifteenth century, there was a concerted effort at Hispanization in Roussillon by the newly centralized Spanish kingdom. The French response, under Louis XIV, was conquest of the region and occupation of Perpignan in 1642. In 1659 the Treaty of the Pyrenees annexed northern Catalonia to France for good. There was little opposition to the Revolution in the region.

Alsace had no political unity before its acquisition during the eighteenth century. Strasbourg was a free city; the Décapole, a federation of towns on the Alsatian plain, were part of the Holy

Roman Empire; the city of Mulhouse was part of the Swiss Confederation. In principle, Louis XIV acquired control over the greater part of Alsace according to the terms of the Treaty of Westphalia in 1648. But this control remained theoretical until after 1680. As with many other territories, Alsace remained free according to the terms of the treaty of annexation, but the intendants nonetheless worked to impose royal taxation and administration. These infractions were not met by any dramatic resistance. The Revolution was welcomed in Alsace, even though the hostility of Jacobinism to the Germanic dialect was not. Three of Napoleon's greatest generals, Kléber, Kellermann, and Rapp were Alsatian. Alsace remained attached to France but linguistically German from then until the Franco-Prussian War (Maugué, 1970: 19ff.).

The first French occupation of Corsica occurred in the eighth century under Pepin, but until the end of the eighteenth century the island was mostly under Genoese control. An egalitarian peasant rebellion against Genoa erupted under Sambucuccio in 1358. This rebellion is strongly reminiscent of the more or less contemporaneous growth of Lollardy in England. This type of "primitive rebellion" continued long after in the form of banditry. There had been several more rebellions during the early eighteenth century, but in 1755 the greatest to date broke out, led by the illustrious Pascal Paoli. Although Paoli never completely succeeded in controlling all of the island, Corsican activists are proud to point out that this revolution and its constitution antedated both the French and the American revolutions. It was a short-lived republic, however, because France acquired control from Genoa in 1768 and defeated Paoli at the Battle of Ponte Novo. During the Revolution, Paoli represented Corsica at the Convention, but under attack by the Jacobins he placed the island under British protection in 1793. In 1796, the French retook Corsica for the last time, and from then on it was part of France. This annexation was certainly sealed by Napoleon Bonaparte's being of Corsican origin.

Philip Augustus first established French power in Flanders, but this was lost in the Hundred Years' War. In spite of the conquest by Louis XIV and the annexation of parts of the region by the Treaty of Nijmegen in 1678 and Utrecht in 1713, at the time of the Revolution, French power in Flemish territory was essentially limited to Lille, Dunkerque, and the Pas-de-Calais. Flanders was conquered by the revolutionary armies and occupied by the troops of the Coalition between 1815 and 1819. It was not until after then that the present boundaries of France in this area were established. The relative paucity of Flemish speakers in French territory indicates that this was one of the least successful areas of French expansion.

2. ETHNIC ACTIVISM FROM THE REVOLUTION TO LIBERATION

The history of ethnic activism from the Revolution until the morrow of World War II is composed of two shorter periods, that prior to World War I and that between the wars. Though the degrees of intensity of ethnic activism in the regions varied considerably during these periods, they had generally the same characteristics. In the first, the political stance was essentially royalist, but during the second there was a growing tendency toward fascism. During both appeared cultural and literary societies that were often, but not always, latently political.

Some of the developments of French political history in general help to explain the changes in ethnic activism. One was the retention of departments by the restored monarchy in 1815; the centralization and standardization of the nation was thus tacitly endorsed by the Bourbons. During the Orleanist monarchy and the Second Empire, no political party offered decentralization, federalism, or any other ideology that endorsed the aims of provincial particularism. During this period, accordingly, ethnic activism was basically romantic and apolitical.

After the establishment of the Republic in 1871, the growing identification of Paris with anticlericalism, antiroyalism, and antiprovincialism led to the formation of a clerical, royalist, provincial alignment that, although it never gained political power, remained a formidable force in French politics. During this time, ethnic activism therefore tended to be royalist.

In the interwar period, measures were undertaken by the Radical Socialist Premier Edouard Herriot in the 1920s to stamp out ethnic languages in the French educational system. This and the increasing domination of Paris by parties of the left led to a drift of ethnic activists toward fascism. The exceptions to this tendency were the Basques and Catalans, whose enemy in the 1930s was not so much socialism in Paris as fascism in Spain.

Virtually the only Occitan activism during either of these two periods was the literary renaissance of Provençal culture known as the Félibrige, led by the poet Frédéric Mistral. Provençal romanticism was part of the large romantic movement in European literature of the same time. During the 1830s, Provençal poetry came into vogue in northern France. Mistral's first influential poem appeared in 1859, and the poet himself died in 1914. These can be taken as the approximate time limits of the Félibrige (Lafont, 1974: 66). Though at first hardly political, Mistral believed in a vague sort of Girondin federalism. He received little sympathy from his republican audience, and after 1870 he became both more political and more conservative. He was shocked by the Paris Commune, by atheism, and by anticlericalism. In general, the Félibrige can be considered as a sort of literary nationalist movement, aiming at restoration of a glorious past culture, but whose political aspects were only secondary.[4] Involvement in the Félibrige did prove politically formative for some of its followers, however. One of the best known of these was Charles Maurras, whose subsequent extreme-right activity is well known.[5]

In addition to the conservative Félibrige, there was an episode connected with the vintners' revolt of 1906, which some have called the "red Félibrige." The revolt was part of widespread labor violence in France at the time, but one of the leaders, Ferroul, who was mayor of Narbonne, linked the wine growers' struggle with that of the Cathari against the northern invaders. He gave speeches in Occitan to crowds who spoke and carried placards in Occitan dialect (Lafont, 1974: 93-94).[6] But the red Félibrige was only an isolated phenomenon.

From 1900 until Liberation, use of the Occitan dialects declined in the countryside and nearly vanished in the cities. Not only was there a concerted government effort to wipe out regional dialects; speaking Parisian French became identified with social mobility, and speaking local patois with stupidity and backwardness. Occitan was preserved and studied by only a handful of linguists and scholars. This lack of cultural awareness meant that until after World War II, there was essentially no Occitan activism after the Félibrige.

By far the most intense ethnic activism between the Revolution and the Liberation was reached in Brittany. This activity, by religious cultural, lay cultural, and political organizations, was so extensive that what follows can only be a summary.[7]

Breton political activity during the nineteenth century was carried on in the Breton Association (Association Bretonne), which was twice formed (1829 and 1834) and suppressed. Cultural activity was the business of the Bardic Academy (Académie Bardique), which began Celtic studies at its foundation in 1855. As for popular agitation, there was none, to all intents and purposes. During the Franco-Prussian War, Breton troops were isolated in the Camp of Conlie, poorly fed and poorly housed, from which many died of disease. The mutinous situation was at least partially caused by the disesteem in which Bretons were held by the military command. But it was not a popular revolt.

Around the turn of the century, the pace of Breton activism, both cultural and political, accelerated. In 1898, the Breton Regionalist Union (Union Régionaliste Bretonne) was formed, a moderate group that wanted teaching of Breton restored in schools, preservation of folk customs, restoration of some Breton autonomy, and some economic aid to the region. Around the same time a druidical organization was founded, the Gorsedd, whose aim was to reestablish what they saw as the true Breton religion. The more conventionally religious Heath Flower (Bleun-Brug), whose purpose was cultural, religious, and scholastic, was founded in 1905 (Serant, 1971: 245). But the most important group, the Breton Nationalist party (Strollad Broadel Breiz) was founded shortly before World War I, in 1911. It was the first Breton separatist party of modern times.

World War I put an end to these activities for the duration of hostilities, but they resumed immediately after the Armistice. A representative of the Breton Regionalist Union delivered a petition to the Versailles Conference to request that, in accord with Wilsonian doctrine, the Bretons be given the right to speak and teach their own language. It was greeted with silence.

During the interwar period, squabbling was constant within the Breton movement, producing a multiplicity of groups. The reasons for these quarrels resided in the splits in French society in general—left vs. right, Catholic vs. anticlerical—and cleavages peculiar to Brittany—separatism vs. regionalism, Breton speakers vs. French speakers. About the Breton movement of the time, a Breton historian has written this description:

> They were of disparate ages, conditions and opinions, like a hotel: the worker rubbed shoulders with the squire, the freemason with the country priest, the communist with the Maurassien; in the annual congresses an elegy on "our dear traditions" came after a Marxist speech; one cited Lenin, another Leo XIII; angelic old men in velvet vests cut short talk about the class struggle by asserting that when Brittany had achieved her liberty again as in the good old days of the Duchess, rich and poor would embrace each other. (Lebesque, 1970: 163)

The most important of the many groups was the Breton Autonomist party (Parti Autonomiste Breton), which published a journal, *Brittany Forever (Breiz Atao)*, and the party came to be known by the Breton name of the journal. The precipitating event of its founding in 1927, by Olier Mordrel and Fanch Debeauvais, was the prosecution of Alsatian autonomists by the government. Other organizations included Breton in School (Ar Brezoneg er Skol), founded around the same time, and a periodical, *The Sickle (Ar Falz)*, founded by the Communist Yann Sohier.

The latent divisions in the Breton movement erupted in 1932. A year earlier, Catholic conservatives had split from the Breton Autonomist party and established the Breton Integral Nationalist party (Parti Nationaliste Breton Intégral), and a similar group broke away soon after, the Breton Nationalist Christians (Nationalistes Bretons-Chrétiens). In 1932, the nationalists succeeded in gaining control of the Breton Autonomist party, and renamed it the Breton Nationalist party (Parti Nationaliste Breton—PNB). A federalist faction broke away from the PNB, and yet another faction within the PNB began a bombing campaign, that lasted for the next few years under the name Black and White (Gwenn ha Du), Brittany's national colors. There was also regular electoral activity outside the Breton Nationalist party, and in 1936 a Breton Front was formed as a response to the Popular Front, composed of the Breton Regionalist Union, the Gorsedd, the Heath Flower, and the Breton Association. Fifteen of their forty-one candidates were elected (Fortier, 1971: 92ff.).

Though they did not attract any substantial following, the bombings and increasingly fascistic tone of the Breton Nationalist party provoked more and more official hostility. After a group of PNB storm troopers staged a forbidden march in 1938, Mordrel and Debeauvais were arrested, and a law against separatist organizations was passed that is still in effect and in use.[8] At the end of August 1939, as war with the Third Reich loomed, the Breton Nationalist party and Brittany Forever were banned.

Mordrel and Debeauvais fled to Nazi Germany, whence they had received intimations that a separate Breton state might be favored. From their office in Berlin, they published a manifesto that read, in part:

> Our countrymen should consider themselves released from any obligation with regard to France. Their actions should aim only at setting up a Breton force which will give back to us control over ourselves and our right to live. (Sérant, 1971: 278)

When the Wehrmacht invaded, they tried to recruit Breton prisoners, who had been segregated at special camps, into military units on the side of Germany. Although the vast majority repudiated these offers, fewer than 150 returned to Brittany with Mordrel and Debeauvais. They were formed in 1941 into the Breton Army (Lu Brezon). A Breton National Council was established in 1940 under German auspices, but the terms of the armistice with Vichy preserved France's borders—aside from Alsace and Lorraine—and so the Council was never more than symbolic. After Abbé Perrot, the founder of the Heath Flower, was assassinated in 1943 by soldiers of the Resistance, the Breton Army was renamed the Perrot Legion (Bezenn Perrot), under the leadership of Célestin Lainé. These troops were under the military command of the Germans, wore Waffen SS uniforms, and participated in reprisal raids against the Resistance. As the Allies advanced, the Perrot Legion retreated to Germany. During the "settling of accounts" in Brittany, some eight hundred collaborators were executed, though it is not certain how many of these were Breton nationalists (Sérant, 1971: 306).

Breton activism during the war, however, was not the exclusive province of collaborators and fascists. In the Free French Forces was an association called Brittany Arise (Sav Breiz). Still, after Liberation the identification of Breton nationalism with the Third Reich was very strong in the public mind.

There has been essentially no Basque autonomist activity in France from the Revolution until the present. The principal reason was that the Basque cultural renaissance took place in Spain in the latter part of the nineteenth century, and French Basques looked across the Pyrenees for nationalist inspiration. When the Basques were granted limited autonomy during the brief life of the Spanish Republic, no answering call for autonomy came from their brothers in France. During the Civil War, the primary aim of French Basques was to help in the struggle against Franco, and, after the victory of the Fascists, to care for the hundreds of thousands of refugees who fled to France. Basque activism in France appeared only when the fight against Franco sharpened after 1960.

Ethnic activism in Catalonia between the Revolution and World War II was rather more vigorous. During the nineteenth century, a modest literary and cultural revival derived from the same romantic spirit as the Félibrige. The Society of Catalan Studies (Société d'Etudes Catalanes), established in 1906, had the same backward-looking stance. This society disappeared during World War II, but in the 1920s, several Catalan literary reviews appeared. In 1937, a youth group was founded, with a more politically oriented magazine, *Our Land* (*Nostra Terra*). But the main preoccupation of the Catalans of Roussillon was with the fate of Spanish Catalonia and the refugees who fled in 1939. World War II brought these activities to an end (Bernardo, 1976: 15-16).

No anti-French autonomist activity went on in Alsace between the Revolution and 1870 when, along with Lorraine, it was detached from France and annexed to Germany. In 1872, in fact, some five thousand persons emigrated from these areas to France in order to retain their citizenship. But this period of German domination was to have serious subsequent ramifications. There was an anti-German autonomist movement in Alsace, and in 1877 five of their candidates were elected to the Diet. The Reich was not able to exert the kind of rigid, central rule that the French had, and the pressure of the Alsatian autonomists led, in 1911, to their being granted their own legislature and a measure of regional autonomy.

In 1918, Alsace was returned to France without a plebiscite, violating the Wilsonian principle of self-determination, as autonomists were later to claim. The overwhelming majority of Alsatians welcomed being rejoined to France, but an active and vocal autonomist minority appeared in the 1920s. The precipitating factors of this activity were attempts by the Herriot government to enforce the Law of Separation of Church and State—passed while Alsace was not part of France, in 1905—and attempts to root out the use of ethnic languages among school children. The first was abandoned because of the animosity it aroused, but the latter was not. Alsatians felt they were able to be good Frenchmen while speaking a language other than French in their everyday lives, but because Parisians failed to understand this, signs saying, "It's chic to speak French," appeared in Alsatian towns.

The autonomist activity was focused in three tiny groups, the leftist Alsatian Progress party (Elsassische Fortschrittspartei), the federalist Regional Party (Landes partei), and the nationalistic Alsace-Lorraine Homeland Union (Elsass-Lothringer Heimatbund).

Each of these parties spawned a number of publications. The government response was not long in coming. In 1928, twenty-two activists were indicted for a supposed plot. Seven of them fled, and of the fifteen tried at the Colmar Trial, four were found guilty and sentenced to a year in prison and five years' exile from Alsace. Such a public outcry arose that three were soon pardoned and the fourth freed anyway. During the rest of the interwar period, Alsatian activism was virtually nonexistent, the war on the Alsatian dialect in schools was relaxed, and the churches and parochial schools still benefited from state support ensured by the Napoleonic Concordat. Then too, the rise of Nazism across the Rhine made membership in the French nation highly desirable by comparison.

During World War II, Alsace was again made part of Germany. In some ways the occupation was more difficult for Alsatians than for other Frenchmen, because, though the others were subject to forced labor service, the former were actually conscripted into the Wehrmacht and sent, for the most part, to Russia. In spite of intense opposition, compliance was forced by holding parents responsible for their sons' conscription. One hundred and thirty thousand were drafted, of whom more than 30,000 were killed. The fact that some Alsatian conscripts were enlisted in the Waffen SS led to their being present at the reprisal massacre of Oradour-sur-Glane in the Midi (Maugué, 1970: 111-125). In general, although the Germans tried to use autonomists for their purposes, most of those who became collaborators and Nazis during the occupation were not autonomists.

During the nineteenth century there was no Corsican activism, cultural or political. The banditry that had always been endemic in the interior continued, and, though it may have had some Paolist inspiration, it was not directed against the French government except for any unfortunates who happened to become its victims. The most that could be said of it politically is that it was "primitive rebellion." [9] During 1910 and 1911, demonstrations were held in Bastia against the high cost of importations to the island, which were subject to government regulation, but this protest was more practical than motivated by ethnic feeling.

During the interwar period, an autonomist movement did appear. In 1920, two brothers named Rocca founded a separatist periodical called *A Muvra*. Two years later they and handful of people founded the Corsican Action party (Partitu Corsu d'Azzione), which was more regionalist than separatist at first, demanding "a government of the island by conscious representatives of the land, under the protection of our great sister nation: France" (Desjardins, 1977: 81). In 1927, its name was changed to Corsican Autonomist party (Partitu Corsu Autonomistu). By 1934, it had gained enough followers to summon six hundred people to an Estates General of Corsica, but at no time during the interwar period did it have more than the most marginal following. One principal reason was that Corsica was a territory claimed by Italian irredentism. Mussolini supported the Rocca brothers, and the identification of autonomism with fascism was enough to keep most Corsicans away. When Corsica was occupied, representatives of the PCA tried to enlist Corsican prisoners of war in the Axis forces, but not one soldier accepted.

If Corsica was an aim of Italian irredentism, Flanders had long been a prize coveted by "greater German" irredentism. During the nineteenth century, French Flemish consciousness was a romantic and literary current of the elite. The Flemish Committee of France (Comité Flamand de France) was established as a learned society in 1852 by Henri de Cousemaker. After the foundation of the Third Republic, and particularly after the Law of Separation of Church and State, the Committee attracted some pro-church regionalist following. These did not crystallize into a political party until after World War I. Abbé Jean-Marie Gantois and a number of other priests established the Flemish Union of France (Vlaamse Verbond van Frankrijk) in 1924. Initially merely hostile to anticlerical policy emanating from Paris, this tiny group moved closer to the extreme-right Flemish National Union of Belgium.

After the Armistice, the Flemish Union of France resumed activity under the direction of Abbé Gantois, with German consent. It published a literary journal and a weekly news magazine during the Occupation. In 1942, the South Flemish Youth Group was established, along the lines of the Hitler Youth. But unlike the Belgian Flemings, the French Flemings never constituted their own unit in the Wehrmacht. In any case, there was never strong public support for an autonomism that identified itself with Nazism and the forcess of the Occupation (Dejonghe, 1970).

3. THE CONTEMPORARY REVIVAL

The years immediately following World War II were devoid of significant ethnic activism outside the realm of culture and folklore. The academic Institute for Occitan Studies (Institut d'Etudes Occitanes) was set up on 1945, a half-dozen or so Breton language and literary associations at the same time, and the European federalist newspaper, *The Voice of Alsace-Lorraine (La Voix d'Alsace-Lorraine)* in 1953. During the 1950s some small signs of revival appeared. In Occitania, François Fontan left the Institute for Occitan Studies and founded the Occitan Nationalist party (Parti Nationaliste Occitan) in 1959. In Brittany, Yann Fouéré founded the Movement for Breton Organization in 1957. The Committee for Study and Liaison of Breton Interests (Comité d'Etudes et de Liaison des Intérêts Bretons—CELIB) had been formed in 1950, but it was composed of established figures whose main aim was government decentralization rather than ethnic activism. The beginnings of decentralization under the Fifth Republic led to the decline of the CELIB, in any case. The real beginning of the contemporary period of ethnic activism coincided with the final disengagement from Algeria; the movement accelerated after the Days of May in 1968.

Figure I.2, depicting the number of ethnic activist groups founded since 1945, shows the importance of these dates. The groups enumerated include cultural societies as well as explicitly political organizations, and also publications that are not connected to organizations, because many carry on activities that are at least partially political. Some of these are mergers of groups founded prevously, and some vanished soon after their appearance. But dates of foundation nonetheless reveal the significance of 1962 and 1968.[10]

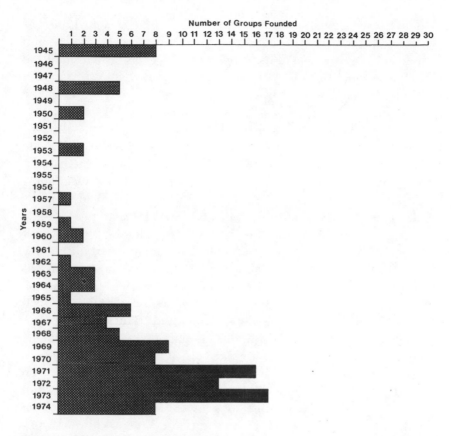

Figure I.2.

As figure I.2 shows, twenty-two groups were founded in the eighteen years between 1945 and 1962. In the six ensuing years, twenty-
two groups were formed, three times as many per year as in the
previous period. And in the six years after 1968, seventy-one groups
were formed, more than three times the rate of the previous six
years. The affect of the end of the Algerian War and the Days of
May is therefore evident.

We need not give a detailed accounting of all the activities of
these groups since 1963, but a sketch of the various directions taken
in each region will depict ethnic activism's nature and intensity.
Having brought its history up to date, we will finish the chapter by
examining the causes of its recent recrudescence.

The latest Occitan movement began in a strike at a coal mine at Décazeville (Aveyron). The strike crystallized regional, union, and ethnic activity, and one of its principal results was formation of the Occitan Committee for Study and Action (Comité Occitan d'Etudes et d'Action—COEA) in 1962 (Lafont, 1974: 271). The COEA formed close links with the Unified Socialist party (Parti Socialiste Unifié), whose ideological stress on *autogestion*—self-management and popular control of industry—meshed well with ethnic autonomism. After 1968, the COEA declined in importance, and a more extreme left formation, Occitan Struggle (Lutte Occitane— LO), under the leadership of Gaston Bazalguès, appeared in its stead. The LO has an artistic arm in the Street Theater (Teatre de la Carriera). These are the elements of the Occitan movement, but it has less important groups as well. The Occitan Socialist party (Parti Socialiste Occitan), established by Robert Allant in 1967, has not grown. The Anarchist-Communist Federation of Occitania (Fédération Anarchiste-Communiste d'Occitanie), begun by Occitan anarchists in 1969, has likewise amounted to little. Young Languedoc (Jeune Languedoc) and Occitan People (Poble d'Oc), founded in 1972, are more conservative, but also have not had great influence (Bazalgues, 1973: 148-149).[11] There are many even smaller groups, such as local chapters of the Institute for Occitan Studies, and electoral groups, such as the Occitan Front (Front Occitan) and We Want to Live on the Land (Volem Viure Al Païs), whose existence has been temporary or influence only local.

A word must be said about the so-called Occitan protest in Larzac. This has been simply a protest against the French army's expansion of a camp to include about 17,000 more hectares of land on a plateau in the Aveyron. The steps toward this expansion took shape in 1971 and 1972, and provoked a reaction from a combination of ecological, antimilitary, union, and student groups. They were also opposed by the owners of farms and businesses who dwell on the plateau designated for absorption. A total of 527 people, according to one estimate, are affected by this expansion, on 107 farms (Kuligowski, 1971: 4ff.).

There is considerable question, though, whether these protests, valid though they may be, are really "Occitan" in the ethnic sense. It is true that one of the well-known Occitan singers, Claude Marti, sang at a protest rally for Larzac in 1972, and that a perennial Occitanist gadfly, Dr. Raymond Bonnafous, is chairman of the Departmental Committee for the Safeguard of Larzac. But close analysis of the situation shows that although it was local and corporatist at the beginning, other regional groups joined it later, and still later it was supported by left-wing Occitan activists. The farmers themselves, who are directly affected by the expansion of the camp, have refused exclusive support from any outside group, and though they assert pride in their local dialect and customs, do not identify with the Occitan movement (Holohan, 1976). It seems that outside groups of many sorts have taken up the Larzac cause, and though it certainly has indigenous support, it is not clear that this is an Occitan issue.

The real beginning of contemporary Breton activism was the offshoot of a young crowd, the Breton Democratic Union (Union Démocratique Bretonne—UDB) from the Movement for Breton Organization in 1963. A related youth group, the Breton Student Youth Group (Jeunesse Etudiante Bretonne) was set up in the same year. The younger militants had an anticapitalist position very similar to that of the Occitan COEA. Their relation with the Unified Socialist Party were also close. They later spawned a far-left group, the Breton Mole (La Taupe Bretonne), which—perhaps intentionally—has not been heard from since. The UDB was and remains the most coherent, organized voice of Breton socialist activism.

The conservative wing of the Movement for Breton Organization was partially preserved in the small Breton National and European Federalist Movement (Mouvement National Breton et Fédéraliste Européen), but part moved toward the Breton Liberation Front (Front de Libération de la Bretagne—FLB). The first wave of bombings by the FLB occurred in the winter of 1967-1968. Even at this time there were divisions within the tiny clandestine group, between more Marxist-oriented guerrillas and nationalists. The fact that the group gave itself two names, the Breton Liberation Front-Breton Republican Army (Front de Libération de la Bretagne-

Armée Républicaine Bretonne—FLB-ARB), was an indication of this division. The network was broken up by the police in 1968. In the following years many bombings occurred, each wave being attributed to an FLB. It is generally recognized that there have been several distinct FLBs.[12] Bombings against property and symbolic government targets occurred in 1971, 1973, and 1975. The pace of the bombings has quickened since then. Ten bombs were detonated by the FLB-ARB in one weekend in January 1978 (*Le Monde,* 17 January 1978), and four during the night of March 5, 1979 (*Le Monde,* 7 March 1979). Generally, the attacks are aimed at offices of the government or utilities, but sometimes the summer houses of particularly wealthy non-Bretons are bombed. Perhaps the most spectacular bombing by Breton terrorists was in a wing of the Palace of Versailles in June 1978, "to protest," said one of the young men who admitted responsibility, "against the humiliation of Breton culture" (*Le Monde,* 2-3 July 1978).

Parallel to these clandestine activities, groups appeared across the spectra of left-to-right and separatist-to-autonomist-to-federalist-to-regionalist. In 1971, the Maoist Breton Communist party (Strollad Komunour Breiz) was established in connection with the second FLB. The Committee for Breton Regional and Progressive Action and Liaison (Comité de Liaison du l'Action Régionale et Progressiste de Bretagne), composed of members of the Unified Union, Union of Socialist Groups and Clubs, and the Breton Student Youth Group, was established in 1969. In the same year a federalist group appeared, the European Committee for the Defense of the Breton People (Comité Européen de Défense du Peuple Breton). Two extreme-left groups appeared in 1972 and 1973, the Breton Action Committees (Comités d'Action Bretons), and the Presses of Breton Anger (Les Rotatives de la Colère Bretonne). The anarchist Breton Resistance (Stourm Breiz) was established in 1974. Finally, in 1975, a shaky coalition, the Breton Socialist Front for Self-Government (Front Socialiste Autogestionnaire Breton) was formed out of the Party of the Land (Strollad Ar Vro), the Breton Action Committees, the Breton Resistance, and the Breton Communist party. But this coalition so far has accomplished little.

Electoral alliances have appeared as well. The Party of the Land presented candidates in eighteen electoral districts in Brittany in the legislative elections of 1973, in cooperation with the European Federalist party. They obtained a little more than 2 percent of the votes (*Le Monde*, 6 March 1973). A moderate Breton Front (Front Breton) ran in the 1968 legislative elections, and its two candidates won 976 and 1,157 votes, respectively (Caerleon, 1971: 219). The Breton Democratic Union presented candidates in fifteen electoral districts in the legislative elections of 1978, in which they obtained slightly less than 2 percent of the vote (*Le Monde*, 14 March 1978).

These are only the outlines of the turbulent and shifting history of the contemporary Breton movement. Some of these groups have never been heard of again. Others, such as the Breton Democratic Union, have a strong organization. Still others are clandestine, so that little can be said for certain about them. There are many other smaller, primarily cultural groups. The definitive account of modern Breton activism remains to be written. Overall, the Breton activists have received little support from the population, except in cultural preservation. The evidence is sparse, but in one study done in 1968, it was clear that although Bretons often define themselves as such in contrast to other Frenchmen, this feeling does not translate itself into political terms (Muzellec, 1973).

The Basque movement has been far simpler and more peaceful. In April 1963, six hundred persons celebrated the Basque national holiday (*Aberri Eguna*) at Itxassou, near Bayonne, and founded Enbata, meaning a wind of freedom. This was a separatist and federalist group, whose aim was a unified Basque nation in a European federation (Héraud, 1966: 216). The principal activity of Enbata, besides publishing a newspaper of the same name, was to support Basque refugees from Spain. Enbata also ran candidates in elections in 1967 and 1968, in which they obtained slightly more than 2 percent of the vote.

There was also a series of violent but small-scale episodes. In 1971, a fracas with the police on Aberri Eguna in Bayonne resulted in the conviction and deportation of two leaders of Enbata to the interior of France. On the same day a year later came another fight with the police. The combination of its explicitly separatist aim and its sporadic confrontations with the police led the government formally to ban the organization in 1974. The newspaper *Enbata* still exists. Little has been heard from several other small Basque organizations, such as the New Century (Mende Berri) and Between Brothers (Anai Artea). The principal activity for French Basques historically has been to provide support for Spanish Basques and occasionally refuge from pursuit. Now that democracy has reappeared in Spain and Basque terrorism has been directed against it, there is considerably less official sympathy for these activities in France. Recently, exiled Spanish Basques have lost the status of political refugees.

The Catalan revival started in 1967, with the formation of the Cultural Group of Catalan Youth (Grup Cultural de la Joventud Catalana) out of an older cultural group; the Roussillon Group for Catalan Studies (Grup Rossello d'Estudis Catalans). In 1969, it changed its name to the Catalan Youth Front (Front de la Joventud Catalana). In the same year, a regionalist and federalist group, the Catalan Regionalist Action (Acció Regionallista Catalana) appeared. Several increasingly leftist groups split away from the Catalan Youth Front in the 1970s. The Roussillon Committee for Study and Animation (Comité Roussillonais d'Etudes et d'Animation) appeared in 1970, the Catalan Socialist Party (Parti Socialiste Catalan) in the same year. The revolutionary and separatist Catalan Workers' Left (Esquerra Catalan dels Traballadores) was established in 1972, the Maoist Roussillon Workers' and Peasants' Left (Gauche Ouvrière et Paysanne Roussillonaise) in 1973. Besides cultural activities and organizing, the actions of these groups have been legal (Bernardo and Rieu, 1973: 303-332; Jaubert, 1974: 313-314). In 1978, candidates appeared in four electoral districts in French Catalonia in the legislative elections. Overall, they received slightly less than 2 percent of the vote *(Le Monde,* 14 March 1978).

The latest Alsatian activism started in 1968, with the foundation of the cultural and literary society, the René Schickele Circle (Cercle René Schickele), named after a distinguished writer in the Alsatian dialect. An alternate press organization, the Alsatian Information Agency (Agence Alsacien d'Information) was set up by some young journalism students in 1970, the same year that saw the foundation of an explicitly political autonomist group, the Regionalist Movement of Alsace-Lorraine (Elsass-Lothringische Föderalistische Bewegung). Politically, this group is relatively conservative, and has made the most consistent electoral efforts. M. Moschenross, a candidate for mayor of Strasbourg, obtained 12 percent of the vote in 1971.

In the next four years, a succession of leftist groups appeared. These were the Alsatian Writers' Council (Conseil des Ecrivains d'Alsace), *Klapperstei 68* (an alternate-press newspaper) in Mulhouse, and Musauer Wäckes (a cultural revolutionary group) in Strasbourg in 1972, the far-left Alsatian Liberation (Libération-Alsace), and the Maoist Peasants of Alsace (Paysans d'Alsace) in 1973. An autogestion-oriented group, finally, was set up in 1974, the Alsatian Cultural Front (Front Culturel Alsacien).

So far, nothing but legal activity has been carried on by Alsatian activists, even though there were allegations of autonomist involvement in an ecologically inspired bombing at Marckolsheim. Autonomist candidates ran in the legislative elections of 1973 (three electoral districts) and 1978 (two electoral districts), in which they obtained about 4.5 percent and 3.5 percent of the votes, respectively *(Le Monde,* 6 March 1973, 14 March 1978). In short, there does not as yet seem to be much popular support for autonomism, although a study in 1972 shows that Alsatians do think of themselves as ethnically distinct. Even though they feel this difference from other Frenchmen, most doubt that the autonomists represent the interests of Alsace (Sondages, 1972: 126-146).

Flanders has seen the mildest activity of all. The principal organization is the cultural Michiel de Swaën Circle (Michiel de Swaën Kring), which was set up by a group of students in Lille in 1972. There is also a Flemish branch of the European Federalist Movement, which began publishing its newspaper, *New Flanders (La Nouvelle Flandre)* in 1970. A cultural association, Hekke-schreeuwen, led to the foundation of a political regionalist group, Thuus Best, in 1977. One candidate of this group ran in a cantonal election in 1976, in which he received 6 percent of the vote.

The Corsican Union (Union Corse) was set up in Paris in 1960. It was a leftist study group whose personnel have come to form the cadres of the more recent groups. The first activist group to appear on the island, the Center for Study and Defense of Corsican Interests (Center d'Etudes et de Défense des Intérêts Corses), appeared in 1964. This group merged with the Corsican Union into the Corsican Regionalist Front (Front Régionaliste Corse) in 1967. An offshoot of the CEDIC, the Corsican Regionalist Action (Action Régionaliste Corse), which eventually was banned and went underground, appeared in the same year.

Since then legal and illegal groups have proliferated in Corsica. As of 6 May 1976, there were four legal groups and seven illegal groups. The former include the Association of Corsican Patriots (Association des Patriotes Corses), established in 1976; the Corsican People's Party for Autonomy (Parti du Peuple Corse pour l'Autonomie); the Corsican Front (Front Corsu), established in 1976; and the Corsican Party for Socialism (Parti Corse pour le Socialisme). The illegal groups include the Corsican Peasant Liberation Front (Front Paysan de Libération Corse), established in 1973; Paoli's Justice (Ghjustizia Paolina), established in 1974; the Committee for Support of the Pentecost Manifesto; the National Liberation Committee; the Corsican Revolutionary Year; the Revolutionary Commandos; and the National Liberation Front, established in 1976. (*Le Monde* 6 May 1976; see also Stagnara, 1976).

Some Corsican activism has been peaceful and electoral. In 1973, a candidate of the Corsican Progress Party (Parti Corse pour le Progrès) obtained 3.4 percent of the vote in the legislative election (*Le Monde*, 6 March 1973). And in 1978, the candidate of the Democratic Alliance for the Future of Corsica (Rassemblement Démocratique pour l'Avenir de la Corse) obtained 7.2 percent of the vote in the legislative election (*Le Monde*, 14 March 1978). But for the most part, Corsican activism has been nonelectoral and illegal.

In fact, Corsican activism has been more violent even than that of the Bretons. Table I.1 indicates the scale and acceleration of this violence:

TABLE I.1

Violent Attacks in Corsica, by Year

Year	Number
1964–70	100
1971	9
1972	18
1973	42
1974	111
1975	226
1976	298
1977	259

SOURCE: *Le Monde*, 7 January 1977; *Le Figaro*, 5 June 1978.

In 1977 alone, there were 246 bombing attempts, 7 armed commando raids, 5 fires, and 30 machine-gun attacks. Only 112 of these were clearly attributed to ethnic activists, though: 19 were claimed by the Corsican Peasant Liberation Front, 61 by the Corsican National Liberation Front, 11 by Corsican Revolutionary Action, 11 by a group called the Balagne Front, and 10 by various other groups *(Le Monde*, 7 January 1977). The frequency of the violence has increased. In 1978 there were about 400 bombings *(Le Monde*, 12 December 1978). In January of that year an important radar base of the French Air Force at Solenzara was occupied and sabotaged by guerrillas of the Corsican National Liberation Front *(Le Monde*, 17 January 1978). In one night in July of 1978, 34 bombs were detonated in Corsica by the FLNC, with the declaration:

Corsican people, tonight our comrades provided once again that we can carry out activities anywhere in Corsican national territory. Once again, the targets represent the presence of French colonialism in Corsica. *(Le Monde*, 6 July 1978)

Though it has a shorter history, Corsican activism is now more violent than, and certainly as vocal as, Breton nationalism.

The government's reaction in Corsica has been similar to its reaction in Brittany. While rigorously pursuing the perpetrators of violence, the government has proposed wide-ranging measures to deal with Corsican problems. On the eve of Prime Minister Barre's visit to the island in 1978, the police arrested more than thirty members of the FLNC, dealing a severe blow to that organization. Meanwhile, the president has proposed a program of economic aid, highway construction, agricultural assistance, educational reform, improved air and sea transportation, and revision of the tax structure *(Le Monde,* 11-12 June 1978). The strategy, which seems to be effective, is to root out the violent while soothing the feelings of the general population.

Table I.2 presents the contemporary ethnic activist groups schematically. The distinctions between the classifications of cultural, regionalist, federalist, autonomist, and separatist are not always clear, and represent differences of emphasis. Autonomists are differentiated from separatists because the latter make a clear declaration that their ethnic territory must be separate from the French state, but the former are not so explicit. Regionalists are differentiated from autonomists, because for the most part their vision of regional emancipation has less of an ethnic than a political dimension—the political emancipation taking place during a revolution or government decentralization. Federalists usually express themselves in terms of European unification. Where it was clear, the stance of these groups in conventional French politics is mentioned; left and extreme left are differentiated because the former generally agreed with the electoral tactics of the Socialists and Communists, whereas the latter see revolution as their goal.

4. THE CONTEMPORARY REVIVAL: CAUSES

In looking at the causes of the contemporary revival of ethnic activism, we are interested in analyzing overall factors common to all of France. In each ethnic region there have been particular

TABLE I.2

Typology of Ethnic Activist Groups in Contemporary France

	Cultural	Regionalist	Federalist	Autonomist	Separatist
Alsace	Cercle René Schickele Conseil des Ecrivains d'Alsace Musauer Wäckes	Comité Libération Mulhouse (*extreme left*) Comité Libération Strasbourg (*extreme left*) Mouvement Régionaliste d'Alsace-Lorraine (*conservative*)	Mouvement Fédéraliste Européen-Region Alsace Parti Fédéraliste d'Alsace-Lorraine	Front Culturel Alsacien (*far left*)	
Flanders	Cercle "Les Amis de la Flandre Française" Hekke-schreeuwen (*left*) Michiel de Swaën Kring		Section Fédéraliste du Pays-Bas Français		

Brittany				
Al Leur Nevez	Comité de Liaison et de l'Action Régionale et Progressiste de Bretagne (*left*)	Comité Européen de Défense du Peuple Breton	Adsav 1532	Front de Libération de la Bretagne
Ar Falz			Jeunesse Etudiante Bretonne	
Ar Skol Dre Lizer	Comités d'Action Bretons (*extreme left*)		Mouvement pour l'Organisation de la Bretagne	
Association des Professeurs de Breton				
Beleien Vreizh	Comité d'Etudes et de Liaison des Intérêts Bretons		Parti Communiste Breton (*left*)	
Bleun-Brug				
Bodadeg Ar Sonerion	Groupe d'Etudes Politiques Bretonnes et Internationales (*extreme left*)		Stourm Breizh (*extreme left*)	
Bretagne Vivante			Strollad Ar Vro	
Cercles de Culture Celtique			Union Démocratique Bretonne (*left*)	
Gorsedd				
Comité d'Action pour la Langue Bretonne (*left*)				

Comité d'Action
pour un Statut
de la Langue
Bretonne

Confédération
des Sociétés
Culturelles
Artistiques et
Folkloriques de
Bretagne

Emgleio Breiz

Jeunesses
Progressistes de
la Bretagne

Kamp
Etrekeltiek Ar
Vrezhonegerion

Kelc'h
Sevenadurel
Gwened

Kuzul Ar
Brezhoneg

French Basque Country	Eskualzaleen Biltzarra, Euskal Gogoa, Euskal Elkargoa, Ikas, Mende Berri, Seaska	Parti Socialiste Basque	Mouvement Fédéraliste Européen Section Basque	Enbata
French Catalonia	Grup Guilhem de Cabestany	Comité Roussillonn-ais d'Etudes et d'Animation (*extreme left*); Gauche Ouvrière et Paysanne Roussillonaise (*extreme left*)		Esquerra Catalana dels Traballadores (*extreme left*)
Occitania	Action Poésie-Occitan (*left*); Les Amis de la Langue d'Oc	Comité Occitan d'Unité Populaire (*extreme left*)		Atelier Occitan Peire d'Auvernha (*left*)
Cinéma Occitan (*left*)				

Comitat Rocabrunenc d'Estudis Occitans (*extreme left*)

Institut d'Etudes Occitanes

Teatra de la Carrera (*left*)

Aparamen

Association per la Defensa dans Arts Occitans (*left*)

Centre Bordelais de Documentation Occitane

Centre Culturel Occitan de l'Etang de Berre (*left*)

Centre Dramatique Occitan

Anarchiste-Communiste d'Occitanie (*extreme left*)

Front Occitan (*extreme left*)

Parti Socialiste Occitan (*left*)

Vida Nostra (*left*)

Centre Régional d'Etudes Occitanes (*left*)

Parti Nationaliste Occitan (*conservative*)

Mouvement Populaire Occitan

Corsica

Union de la Patrie

Front Régionaliste Corse (*left*)

Centre d'Etudes et de Défense des Intérêts Corses

Association des Patriotes Corses

Parti du Peuple Corse pour l'Autonomie

Action pour la Renaissance de la Corse

Front de Libération Nationale de la Corse (*extreme left*)

Front Paysan de Libération de la Corse

Ghjustizia Paolina

Parti Corse pour le Socialisme

33

catalytic events, such as the settlement of former Algerian colonists in Corsica, which we will not look at in detail. The aim here is to find keys to the pattern of ethnic activism in France and in other countries. Three sets of factors lie behind its reappearance. The first derives from increasing participation by France in a worldwide economic system. Second, government policy has helped spur regionalist feeling, and, at the same time, ethnic regionalism. The third set can be described as political, from the processes of decolonization, the examples of other ethnic movements around the world, and the near-revolution of May 1968.

With the postwar participation of France in the European Coal and Steel Community and later the Common Market, the traditional significance of national boundaries has been greatly undermined. Until the formation of these international economic organisms, the nation-state could, at least for propaganda purposes, be described as an economic as well as a political unit. But France is now part of an integrated, worldwide economic system in which the idea of "we" as opposed to "others" is not realistic. All industrialized countries are more interdependent than ever before. Once customs barriers between Western European nations were abolished, as soon as passage from one country to another could be accomplished with little or no formality, the nation-state as a focus of moral principle and emotional attachment was greatly weakened. This change is reinforced by the existence of the North Atlantic Treaty Organization, in which armed forces are integrated on a supranational scale to an extent never before seen. In an age of global alignments, nation-states mean less. The economic and military importance of the nation-states of Western Europe has declined as supranational economic and political systems have emerged. The suppression of regionalism in these nations historically was necessary to maintain unity in the face of hostile neighbors. Now that the neighbors are seen as close cousins, previously suppressed regionalisms are reemerging.

The effects of worldwide economic integration are more specific than a general decline in the nation-state. Instances of ethnic resentment often stem from local industries being taken over by

large, international corporations and then shutting down or periodically halting operations. The strike at Décazeville was the result of
the Paris-based owners of the mine ourtailing operations. This was
one of the first cases in which the phrase "internal colonialism" was
used by commentators and spokesmen. The same militancy erupted
when Wendel Industries, which had taken over the Forges
d'Hennebont, a small metalworking factory in Brittany, shut down
the plant. There are many other cases of large multinational corporations taking over local industrial and agricultural enterprises.
This act is often denounced as "internal colonialism," but is not so
much the lack of industrialization as the integration of a region—
ethnically distinct or not—into a continental and worldwide economic system. The seat of decision-making is farther and farther
removed from the local populace.

Expressing resentment at the effects of his modernization, one
Occitan polemic says, "The few local industries that exist or existed
are closing more and more frequently. They are called 'unprofit-
able. . . .' One could say that there are still some industries—in
Marseille, Toulouse, Montpellier—but they are in the hands of international capital, and are often used as safety valves. If things
aren't going well in Paris or in the Ruhr or in Lyon, they close a
factory in the South" (Rouanet, 1970: 11-12). The Breton equivalent of this lament can be found in Guin (1977: 267-276, 295-304).

Success or lack of success in adapting to the new economic structures can affect whether a region develops a strong autonomist
movement or remains more within the conventional French political dialogue. Chatelain and Tafani argue that rapid modernization
of archaic societies was traumatic both in Brittany and in Corsica,
but that in the former the peasantry managed to adapt by agrarian
syndicalism, and in the latter the traditional power structure has
remained intact. This is why autonomism has relatively little public
support in Brittany, in spite of a very vigorous cultural movement,
whereas it has much more support in Corsica (Chatelain and Tafani, 1976: 19-20).

Regional awareness is not simply the result of external economic
forces. French government policy itself, in several ways, has stimu-

lated it. Chronologically, the first of these measures was passage of the Deixonne Law in 1951, which for the first time gave official sanction to the teaching of ethnic languages in French schools. Article 10 allowed the "facultative teaching of local languages and dialects," specifically Breton, Basque, Catalan, and Occitan (excluding Corsican and Alsatian dialects) in colleges and *lycées*. Because no master's degree was offered in these languages, the law was more a gesture than an encouragement (Calvet, 1974: 183). But it is clear that the law and the debate preceding its passage helped stimulate ethnic consciousness where these languages were spoken.

In quite a different way, efforts at decentralization by the government have helped arouse regional consciousness. As early as the Fourth Republic, there were attempts at counteracting the effects of all decision-making being done in Paris. The work of Gravier (1972) particularly has brought to the public eye the need for decentralization. Serious efforts did not begin until the Fifth Republic, when in 1963 the Commissions for Regional Economic Development (Commissions de Développement Economique et Régional—CODERS) were formed. France was subsequently grouped into regions for planning purposes, which was supposed to counterbalance the relation between the departmental prefect and the Parisian bureaucracy.

In 1972, the CODERS were replaced with a regional council, an economic and social committee, and a regional prefect. The first is composed of deputies, representatives elected by general councils, municipal councils, and urban communities, who advise the regional prefect. The second body is composed of representatives of businesses and unions and cultural groups, but has only a consultative function. Finally, the prefect himself retains all decision-making power, and is appointed in Paris. Thus there has been apparent regionalization but little real decentralization. The very guarded and cautious aspect of this policy has further pointed out the imbalance of power between Paris and the regions. The timidity of the government about decentralization has done as much as the efforts it has made in this direction to contribute to ethnic activism today.

The referendum of 1969 is another example of policy encouraging ethnic awareness. The direct political antecedent to the referendum was the upheaval of 1968. Its avowed purpose was to test peoples' acceptance of mild decentralization and the reform of the process whereby the Senate was chosen. Its real purpose was to test General de Gaulle's popularity following the threat to his government the year before (Williams, 1970: 282-287). The electorate voted down the proposal, 53 percent to 47 percent; the debate that preceded it was lively. As in regionalization, it was less the actual policy changes than the official acknowledgment of their necessity that contributed to the growth of regional feeling.

One action by the head of state may also be cited. In 1967, General de Gaulle, during a state visit to Canada, pronounced the slogan "Long Live Free Quebec" in Montreal. The irony of de Gaulle's partisanship in ethnic autonomy in a foreign country in the face of alleged suppression of ethnic groups was lost on few militants (see, e.g., Lebesque, 1970: Ch. VI). Thus, in many ways that were doubtless uncoordinated and unanticipated—the Deixonne Law, regionalization measures, the referendum of 1969, and General de Gaulle's remarkable outburst—the government itself contributed to the growth of ethnic awareness in France's regions.

One of the most important series of events in this regard was the loss by France of overseas colonial possessions. These included Indochina (1945-1954) and Algeria (1954-1962). The victory of the Vietminh was less important than that of the Algerian National Liberation Front, because no one pretended that Vietnam, Laos, and Cambodia were part of the French nation. The loss of Indochina demonstrated to the world that a determined peasant army could defeat the forces of one of the most industrially advanced countries on earth. This was shocking enough to French national pride, but Algeria had been considered an integral part of the nation since the early days of the Third Republic. No matter that Muslims did not have the same rights as other French citizens; hundreds of thousands of loyal Frenchmen had colonized the Mediterranean rim of the country and their work and organizational ability had made it a highly prosperous agricultural region. The official description of France as "one and indivisible" included Algeria. The fact that in a few years an indigenous guerrilla movement could succeed in detaching part of France was a dramatic lesson.

First, it simply showed that the nation was not so indivisible as it had seemed, and that Breton guerrillas, for instance, might succeed as Vietnamese guerrillas had. It demonstrated too, hard on the heels of the Indochina debacle, the severe limitations on the usefulness of armed forces in imposing a political status rejected by a native population. Finally, the Algerian war itself highlighted the political difference between indigenous groups in France and Paris. Some ethnic activists came to think of themselves as colonized when they perceived the position of the *fellaghas*. Claude Marti says,

> Some of us [Occitan schoolboys] realized that there really was a different kind of culture in Algeria, and that people were being killed all the time there and villages razed to the ground. One day, one of our Algerian friends, Rachid Taieb, said to us, "But it was the same with you people! There was a terrible war against you to impose on you a model of civilization that was not your own!" He was actually telling me my history, to me who neither knew my own history nor his! (Marti, 1975: 70).

Though the FLN showed that it was possible for a small group of militants to wage a successful war of national independence, this was not the only example of militant separatism in the postwar period. The success of the Zionists in Israel, the Mau Mau in Kenya, and other decolonization movements in Asia and Africa had a demonstration effect, that nation-states could be carved out of empires. The less successful but dramatic activity of the Kurds in Iraq and Iran, the Basques in Spain, and the Irish Republican Army in Ulster inspired some to believe that the same could be accomplished in France.

The example of a small and dedicated revolutionary group shaking France to its foundations was given in 1968. Although there is little question that the Days of May were the result of long-standing grievances in the universities, schools, and factories, the outbreak of rebellion was heavily influenced by organized leftist groups. If the Situationists could have such success in formenting university and school rebellion, it was at least possible that similarly organized ethnic activists could have some success.

A measure of ethnic autonomy was promised by the now-defunct Common Program of the Left, the electoral alliance between Communists and Socialists that was formed in 1972. The French Communist party was not friendly to autonomism, attached as it was to the principle of democratic centralism. The Socialist party, however, contains many militants who came from the Unified Socialist party, in which the stress on autogestion favors local and regional control. Again, it was not the success of the program that stimulated ethnic awareness, but the acknowledgment of ethnic activists' demands that aroused their hopes.

To summarize, the contemporary wave of ethnic activism has stemmed from apparently unrelated and heterogeneous factors: economic modernization and international integration, emergence of supranational political entities, government measures to regionalize, the loss of overseas territory, the examples given by other national "liberation" movements, and the fragility of the state as demonstrated in 1968.

5. CONCLUSION

The three periods of ethnic activism in France's post-Revolutionary history have been characterized as royalist, fascist, and leftist. These mutations should not be thought of as a sign of superficiality or hypocrisy. Ethnicity is a social category that cuts across class lines, and is capable of appealing to the interests of any or several of its constituent classes at the same time. This is why it is not correct to characterize ethnic activism as "left" or "right," because it can be both.

The most important reason for these successive changes in ethnic activism's political stance has been the nature of the government in power in Paris. When this government was anticlerical and republican, the ethnic activist response was a romantic sort of Catholic royalism. At those times when Paris was dominated by Socialists and other parties of the left from 1923 to 1926 and 1936 to 1938, ethnic activism drifted toward fascism. Now that Parisian power is wielded by a center-right coalition, the response of the militants is expressed in terms of socialism and a struggle against internal colonialism. If a socialist government should assume power, unless it takes real measures to grant regional autonomy, ethnic activism will probably shift again to the right.

There is something different about the latest phase, though. In neither of the prewar periods did ethnic activism receive much popular support. In the first period, the literary and cultural societies were elite associations that had little in common with the masses. Even if they had not had royalist tendencies, it is unlikely that they could have gained a mass following. During the interwar period, a more fateful mistake was made by the Breton, Corsican, and Flemish autonomists, that of identifying with fascism. This isolated them from the mainstream of democratic sentiment in their regions. One of the clearest differences between prewar and contemporary ethnic activism is that now the movement is systematically attempting to appeal to popular sentiments and interests. Ethnic activism is finally addressing itself to the ethnic groups themselves.

In this chapter we have stressed events and causes unique to France. The rebirth of ethnic activism is a worldwide phenomenon, however. Modernization of previously underdeveloped areas, disrupting long-standing pockets of regional stagnation, is at work wherever ethnic militancy has appeared. Such an ethnic rebirth, however, is totally at odds with the expectations of conventional social scientific theory. In the next chapter we examine theoretical approaches to ethnicity in the past, and contemporary attempts to come to grips with its startling new strength.

CHAPTER TWO

The Problem of Ethnic Activism
in Modern Society

Ethnic activism is a problem in modern society because it defies expectations. Social theorists of the late nineteenth and early twentieth centuries assumed that as societies became more modern, the social relations of capitalism would supersede previous social forms, among which was ethnicity. Modern social theorists, such as structural-functionalists, insofar as they have dealt with ethnicity, similarly consider that it is a primordial sentiment antithetical to modernity. Political theorists of "nation-building" have led us to expect that as social formations are modernized in the framework of nation-states, ethnic differences are supplanted by a homogeneous national consciousness. The appearance of ethnic activism in modern society is therefore an anomaly, an empirical reality that cannot be accommodated by the prevailing pattern of thought in social science (see Kuhn, 1970: 52-65). Very recently, some thinkers are coming to grips with the anomaly. Some have merely pointed it out but others have suggested a theory of internal colonialism, which may in part resolve it.

Few nineteenth-centry social theorists dealt with ethnicity explicitly. The general assumption was that as societies became more modern, social groups based on the capitalist market economy would supersede earlier forms of social organization. The terminology of these categories varied from one thinker to another but the expectation was generally the same. Karl Marx, for instance, saw capitalism cutting through "patriarchal, idyllic relations." Instead of illusions of solidarity and sanctity, capitalism provides no illusions to cover its "naked, shameless, direct, brutal exploitation" (Marx and Engels, 1955: 12). Like the other illusions, ethnicity is a form of false consciousness, to be done away with by the advance of capitalism and class struggle.

Marx's only direct treatment of the phenomenon that we know today as ethnic activism was in his and Engels's comments on the nationalism of minorities. In general, they differentiated between peoples who had a history of existence as a nation, such as the Irish and the Poles, and the "historyless peoples," the *geschichtslosen völker*, who earned nothing but scorn. The former were engaged in a legitimate struggle for national existence, but the latter had no right to it. As Engels wrote in the *Neue Rheinisches Zeitung* in 1849 with regard to the Basques and the Welsh,

> These debris of a nation pitilessly crushed by the advance of history, these rejects of peoples constantly become the fanatical supporters of counterrevolution and will remain so until their complete extermination or denationalization.

Thus in some cases ethnic activism was acceptable and in some cases it was not. The basis of this acceptability was rather circular, because those peoples who already had a history as a nation were the only ones seen to be legitimately aspiring to nationhood.

Marxists subsequently preserved this ambiguity about ethnic nationalism. Around the turn of the century, the Austro-Marxists, led by Bruno Bauer, considered ethnic nationalism to be potentially progressive. He thought that a people's right to "decide for itself concerning its state organization" should be supported by the social democrats. On the other hand, Rosa Luxembourg's scorn for dreams of Polish independence was reminiscent of Engels's opinion of the Basques and the Welsh. In her view, Polish independence was a utopian and reactionary idea, because it was "contradictory to the interests of capitalism" (Haupt et al., 1974: 232, 202).

Marxists have been ambivalent about ethnic activism, because on the one hand there was the conception of nationality as a pre-capitalist social formation, which would be "crushed" by history. On the other hand, some nationalist movements, such as the Polish, were potentially strong allies in the struggle against reactionary governments. Tactically speaking, such movements are useful but suspect, not only because ethnicity is outdated, but also because the nation-state to which they aspire is supposed to be a bourgeois creation (cf. Enloe, 1973: 42-43).

Max Weber's treatment of ethnicity was somewhat incidental, but he shared the expectation that class relations would conquer as capitalism spread, even though he did not agree that class relations were necessarily hostile. Weber differentiates between class and status, the former derived from a person's or a group's position in the rational exchange relations of the marketplace. The latter are nonrational, ascriptive categories. The belief in common ethnic identity is artificial, according to Weber, which produces a sense of communality and solidarity "if rationally regulated action is not widespread." This communal consciousness "takes the form of a brotherhood on the basis of the belief in common ethnicity" (Weber, 1968: 389). Because modernization and rational, market-oriented action are coextensive, ethnicity declines as modernity prevails.

Emile Durkheim treats the change from traditional to market-oriented society differently, referring instead to the supersession of mechanical solidarity by organic solidarity. The growth of the division of labor breaks down smaller segments of society and integrates them into a whole. At the same time, "dialects and jargons begin to resolve themselves into one and the same national language" (Durkheim, 1964: 187). Although Durkheim does not directly refer to ethnic groups, they are included in his expectations about "dialects and jargons."

Marx, Weber, and Durkheim are not the only classical social theorists, but it would be superfluous to cite more. In view of the similarity of ideas among thinkers who otherwise diverge so strongly, it is not surprising that this perspective on the relation between modernization and ethnicity should have persisted well into the twentieth century. Both structural-functionalism and the theories of nation-building expect an inverse relation between modernity and ethnic indentification.

Talcott Parsons's comments on ethnicity can be taken as representative of the school of structural-functionalism. He thinks of an ethnic group as "an aggregation of kinship units" who believe they are of common descent. But as the division of labor increases and the institutions of the market and private property spread, a more advanced type of social organization develops. This more advanced society is, in Parsonian terms, "qualitatively new" (Parsons, 1968: 172, 173, 176). Evidently ethnicity belongs to an earlier, premodern type of society, and he expects that as societies become more modern, ethnicity will decline.[1]

The relation between modernization and subnational ethnic groups has also been treated by political scientists attempting to predict the course of nation building in the emerging states, most of which are former colonies. They were generally expected to follow a course similar to that of the nation-states of Western Europe. In the latter, modernization and nation forming had apparently worked in tandem. One of the essential features of nation forming was suppression of regional ethnic identities and substitution for them of a sense of nationhood among all peoples within the territorial confines of the state.

Karl Deutsch, for example, considers the assimilation of minorities to be part of his all-important process of mobilization, which in turn in is a correlate of modernization. Mobilization goes hand in hand with the spread of markets, industries, cities, and mass communication, and is "a decisive factor in national assimilation or differentiation" (Deutsch, 1953: 162; see also 1961). Lucian Pye, similarly, implies that modernization and political development accompany one another. Political development includes, among other things, "mass mobilization and participation," national identification as opposed to ethnic, tribal, or other forms of subnational identification (Pye, 1966: 33-45). Other examples of the expectation that modernization produces national integration can be found in Almond and Powell (1966, esp. 299-332) and Kautsky (1976: 25-34). Although the primary concern of these thinkers is substitution of state nationalism for ethnic or tribal consciousness by the processes of modernization in the Third World, their expectations are based on what now appears to be a mistaken premise. For ethnic activism has reemerged in precisely those nation-states which had been considered models for the new nations, Great Britain and France.

These expectations have recently been subjected to criticism and review. In political science, Parenti (1967) and Miller (1971) are two such critics. Eisenstadt (1971) has listed a series of possible permutations between the variables of modernization and nation-building that show varieties of association between stages in each. And Heeger says that, "Social change . . . may only further fragment the already fragmented new nation-state" (Heeger, 1974: 6). There have been parallel reassessments of expectations about ethnicity's demise in advanced capitalist societies, such as those by Glazer and Moynihan (1963), Fishman (1966), and Novak (1971). These works deal with the persistence of ethnic identification in the atypical case, the United States, but their relevance for the theoretical problem is clear.

There have also been attempts to reconsider the relation between modernization and ethnic identification more generally, focusing on modern societies in which ethnic groups are indigenous and regionally based. One of the most incisive of these is that of Enloe. Her basic question was whether modernization inevitably leads to decline in ethnic community. Her conclusion was that there may not be an inverse relation between the two, and there may be no relation at all. Ethnic identification satisfies a psychological need that persists through various types of society. "Thus ethnicity survives long after its traditional functions have been taken over by more impersonal, secular groups" (Enloe, 1973: 268), Connor (1972, 1975), and DaSilva (1975) also question the relation between modernization and the eclipse of ethnicity.

Another recent idea is that ethnic groups have always existed within and between classes. They are now reemerging in advanced industrial societies because of the decline in bitterness of class conflict there. As long as the struggle over scarce resources was one in which the gain of one side was the loss of the other, class interest tended to suppress or subordinate other solidarities. In wealthy countries, where even the poorest citizens are comparatively well off, ethnicity has been able to reemerge (Heisler, 1974; Berger, 1972). Glazer and Moyihan argue that this makes ethnicity a powerful political tool. It has affective ties that are more effective than class in making demands for the goods and services of the welfare state (Glazer and Moynihan, 1975).

In all these criticisms, there was no attempt to advance a comprehensive theory for explaining the resurgence of ethnic activism in advanced industrial society. So far, only one systematic attempt of this sort has been made, in the theory of internal colonialism.[2] This concept is derived from the Marxist perception of the effects of uneven capitalist development. Lenin (1956), Gramsci (1959), and Nairn (1974), for instance, study the effects of uneven capitalist development in Russia, Italy, and Scotland. In each, uneven development meant that ethnic minorities were relegated to a kind of colonial status within the larger society. Often the nationalism of these minorities was the expression of regional bourgeoisies whose aspirations to political autonomy were a means of achieving parity with majority business classes or freedom from the anachronistic rule of the aristocracy that controlled the state. Bourgeois ethnic nationalism attempts to mobilize other classes within the ethnic group to gain legitimacy, and therefore develop romantic literature about the earthy virtues of the people (cf. Nairn, 1974: 64). Uneven development and the preservation of underdeveloped ethnic enclaves within capitalist society are the underlying causes of ethnic nationalism. This is the germ of the theory of internal colonialism.

One of the first to use the phrase was Mills, in his discussion of uneven development in Latin America and other countries of the Third World. He says that the developed parts of these countries are "imperialist powers" in relation to the undeveloped parts, which are internal colonies (Mills, 1962: 152). Horowitz also uses the phrase in refering to Third World countries, but not to ethnic regions (Horowitz, 1972: 22; see also Nolasco-Armas, 1971). In his much more elaborate articulation of the way internal colonialism operates, Gonzalez-Casanova does argue that it can preserve ethnic regions. According to him, internal colonialism "corresponds to a structure of social relations based on domination and exploitation among culturally heterogeneous, distinct groups. . . ." The relations between the urban and rural parts of underdeveloped societies are colonial, "because cultural differences between the city and the country are acute" (Gonzalez-Casanova, 1965: 33; see also Stavenhagen, 1965). It is clear that these formulations of internal colonialism are not meant to be applicable to ethnic relations in modern societies.

To explain ethnic relations in modern capitalist society, Hechter provides both a theoretical framework and a description of internal colonialism in a single case. His formulation is worth quoting at length, because it is so clearly expressed, and because paraphrase might distort or oversimplify:

The spatially uneven wave of modernization over state territory creates relatively advanced and less advanced groups. As a consequence of this initial fortuitous advantage, there is crystallization of the uneven distribution of resources and power between the two groups. The superordinate group, or core, seeks to stabilize and monopolize its advantages through policies aiming at the institutionalization of the existing stratification system. It attempts to regulate the allocation of social roles such that those roles commonly defined as having high prestige are reserved for its members. Conversely, individuals from the less advanced group are denied access to these roles. This stratification system, which may be termed a cultural division of labor, contributes to the development of a distinctive ethnic identification in the two groups. Actors come to categorize themselves and others according to the range of roles each may be expected to play. They are aided in this categorization by the presence of visible signs, or cultural markers, which are seen to characterize both groups. At this stage, acculturation does not occur because it is not in the interests of institutions at the core. (Hechter, 1975: 9).

He examines the applicability of this model to the "Celtic fringe" in British national development from 1536 to 1966, but clearly it is applicable elsewhere. His formulation states the theory consistently enough to enable us to draw hypotheses from it.

There are some problems with the phrase itself, however. The first is the term "colonialism." Strictly speaking, a colony is formed by sending settlers from a mother country to settlements in another country. A colony is thus the result of more or less organized expeditions to areas that may or may not be inhabited by natives, and consists of communities of these settlers that remain cohesive and solidary. In this sense there were attempts at colonization of previously uninhabited areas in France during the Middle Ages (cf. Bloch, 1964: 9-11), but there is little correspondence between areas of France colonized in this fashion and the parts of France that could be called internal colonies in the sense meant by Hechter. True colonization was carried out by the French, but in Algeria, not in the mother country itself. A better term might be "imperialism," because in this type of system little attempt is made to send settlers to subordinated territories. But this term is unacceptable, because imperial systems have otherwise been so heterogeneous that it would confuse more than enlighten, and because the word has too many value-laden associations.

"Internal colonialism" has been used to describe the situation of blacks in the United States (Carmichael and Hamilton, 1967; Staples, 1976; Cruse, 1968; Tabb, 1970; Allen, 1969), and of other minorities as well (Blauner, 1972; Almaguer, 1975; Lott, 1976; Moore, 1974; Barrera, 1972. Others have depicted it as identical with uneven economic development in the United States (Gorz, 1971; Luke, 1978; Webb, 1971). None of these applications is relevant for the case of France or Western Europe. In these instances it is used as a polemical label for relations that can be more accurately and prosaically described as either racial and ethnic subordination or regional inequality. Because virtually all American ethnic groups are urbanized, and hence not regionally based, and because all but one are composed of the descendants of voluntary immigrants, internal colonialism is a term of little scientific utility for describing the situation in the United States. In short, it clouds more than it clarifies.

As for its application to Europe, it is still fraught with difficulties of definition even in that empirical context. Some French activists have used it with little care for theoretical precision. Lebesque (1970) talks of Brittany as an internal colony, but he talks more of the psychological effects of colonization than of its processes. Marti says the same of Occitania (Marti, 1975: 69-71). Neither provides a clear formulation of what internal colonialism is. Other activists point out structural aspects of French society as illustrations, and it is worth looking at some of these analyses to get a picture of the varieties of meaning the phrase has acquired in France.

In talking of the strike at Décazeville in 1962, Lafont writes,

> It was a "regional strike": the peasants and small merchants of Aveyron supported the strike. It was an Occitan strike: the miners were Occitans who sang in their language and even wrote in it. . . . The *Nouvel Observateur* wrote of the revolt of the internally colonized. The term "internal colonialism" was already being used in Occitan circles. (Lafont, 1974: 271).

What did the Occitan militants mean by this term? Rouanet (1970) has written a political commentary on the poetry and song of the current Occitan movement. The poetry is pungent, and it is not surprising that the author uses the image of internal colonialism as a description of the Occitan condition. Occitania is colonized by

arms, it suffers from "fiscal colonization, administrative colonization," from mental colonization, and from economic colonization.
She describes the latter:

> Thirty-two departments south of the Loire are more and more
> overshadowed by underdevelopment. The countryside is being
> depopulated. Villages are dying, towns are stagnating and suf-
> focating. Farmers are giving up or will give up and die, faced
> with competition from the great, producers of the North or
> governmental measures. . . . This is a typically colonial fact:
> raw materials are not used where they come from, and do not
> supply the industry in the area where they are extracted: the
> gas from Lacq, bauxite, sea salt, silver ore, hydroelectric
> power, wine, petroleum, go elsewhere to be refined. (Rouanet,
> 1970: 12)

The first part of the passage indicates that for this author, internal
colonialism is a consequence of urbanization and modernization.
There is an implicit contradiction in the description. A truly underdeveloped region would be so economically stagnant that there
would be no depopulation of the countryside. If, as Rouanet says,
the countryside in Occitania is being depopulated, this is a sign of
economic change rather than stagnation. As French agriculture
modernizes and becomes integrated into the Common Market,
large agricultural enterprises undercut and drive out small family
farms. This is a well-known feature of French economic development, and was delayed as long as it was by the policy of agricultural protectionism that has been sacred since the Meline Tariff of
the 1890s. The "rural exodus" of the last twenty-five years is actually the result of modern agricultural practices finally having their
effect upon rural France.

What the author means is clearly shown in the second part of the
passage. Internal colonialism does not really mean underdevelopment, it seems. It really means national integration and centralization, in which the products of one region are consumed in another,
in which the centers of decision-making are removed farther and

farther from the local people. In this analysis, then, internal colonialism refers to modernization and the processes it entails: decline in the agricultural population, increase in urban population, increase in intranational and international interdependence, consolidation of enterprises into larger national and multinational corporations. The use of the term by Rouanet is clearly one that blames Occitan oppression on the modern world. It is thus a reactionary formulation in the purest sense of the word.

A class-based analysis is presented by Atelier Occitan Peire d'Auvernha (n.d.). Their contention is that the "centralist state" has always opposed ethnic languages because of the class characteristics of those who speak them:

> Because in Occitania, Occitan is only spoken by the popular classes, the result is that most of the time there can only be, for whomever speaks it, social mobility or promotion in his profession if he ceases entirely to use it. (Atelier Occitan Peire d'Auvernha, n.d.: 7)

They provide extensive documentation of the low average incomes in the Occitan departments compared to income in Paris. This purports to illustrate how Occitania is an internal colony.

This use of the term, then, is rather different from that of Rouanet. First, it argues that internal colonialism is explicitly an instrument of ethnic oppression, because the "popular classes" speak the ethnic language, and that hostility to this language is the result of upper-class antagonism to those who speak it. Second, it argues that the low incomes in Occitania in comparison to Paris are proof of the oppression of ethnically distinct Occitans by French speakers of the north.

These arguments are not only refuted but demolished by Chevalier (1972). He does not argue with the statistics presented by the militants. He argues that what they call internal colonialism is really nothing but interdependence and regional specialization. As he writes,

The mistake they make is that they have systematically given an ethnic, and even nationalist, interpretation to facts that are true of most great centralized states. Nearly all the aspects pointed out concerning the Occitan areas can in fact be found in the Northern part of France as well, notably in the regions which did not undergo the great industrial expansion of the 19th and 20th centuries. (Chevalier, 1972: 374)

It is quite true, he says, that the "popular classes" speak Occitan, but this shows that the Occitan militants are themselves elitists. The people who speak Occitan do not read it, and Occitan activism "seems to be the action of a handful of revolutionary militants and teachers as isolated from the masses as are the elite" (Chevalier, 1972: 377).

To restate Chevalier's refutation succinctly, there are more and less developed areas in France, but among the less developed are those which are ethnically distinct and those which are not. The percentage of the active population that is engaged in agriculture is quite high, but the western departments of Maine-et-Loire and Vendée also have large agricultural sectors, and they are not ethnically distinct. In other words, two of France's ethnic regions are among the most economically developed areas of the country, Alsace and Flanders. Although they are ethnically distinct—particularly Alsace—they are heavily industrialized.

One of the most sophisticated uses of the term is in the Marxist-Leninist analysis of Frères du Monde (1971). They concede that there is no relation between the centralization of the French state and the existence of regional underdevelopment in France. Capitalist expansion has not brought about the existence and dimensions of the nation, nor has underdevelopment been brought about by centralization of the government. After all, the dimensions of France were established long before the expansion of capitalism as an economic system. They do argue, however, that as the capitalist economy increasingly pervades the regions of France, the "underdevelopment of the satellite is the absolute condition of the development of the metropole" (Frères du Monde, 1971: 36).

> It is the concentration of economic activity . . . in the metro-
> pole which brought about the aggravation of the pauperiza-
> tion of the regions. It could do this and nothing else. Since
> Paris had monopolized all power, it became the focal point for
> private investment, national or foreign, and for public invest-
> ment, undertaken through use of fiscal revenue, (Frères du
> Monde, 1971: 37)

It is worth pointing out in passing that this conception of internal
colonialism is at odds with that of Hechter, who thinks of regional
inequality being the result of an "initial, fortuitous" advantage
being exploited by the central power. This analysis, on the other
hand, says that regional "pauperization" is the result of the power
of the central government.

This analysis, however ingenious, suffers from the fact that internal colonialism as thus described does not differ perceptibly from
uneven economic development and regional specialization. They
do not argue that the underdeveloped regions are all ethnically
specific, or that the developed regions are more French; they cannot say this because it is not true. The uneven character of capitalism's spread and that of modernization in general is a process that
has long been recognized. Frères du Monde is putting old wine in
new bottles and giving it an attractive label. All they say, in fact, is
that the peripheral regions in France are relatively less prosperous
than the Parisian region, and that this is the result of processes
inherent in capitalism.

We have considered briefly three examples of how internal colonialism is used by contemporary French activists to describe their
condition. The first considered it as synonymous with modernization and the third presented the same argument in more subtle
terms, that internal colonialism consists of the unevenness of capitalist development. Both of these arguments use internal colonialism as a slogan to provide a moral condemnation of social processes
long known by different names. The second argument was an attempt to assert that there is a connection between ethnic specificity
in France and level of economic development. This is a daring

assertion, but it is simply not true. There are ethnically distinct regions that are poor and some that are relatively rich, whereas some regions not ethnically distinct are just as poor and some are rich.

The fact that there is no relation between a region's distinctiveness and its level of economic development does not mean that the term "internal colonialism" should be discarded, however. Different levels of economic development may be connected to different degrees of ethnic discontent. Internal colonialism does not explain the *origin* of economic differences between regions in France, but it could be related to the *preservation* of some ethnic regions in relatively disadvantaged condition and the resentment, militancy, and violence this discrimination could spawn. In short, internal colonialism might explain levels of ethnic activism even though it does not explain the origins of ethnic differences.

Thus, in spite of its value-laden implications, semantic imprecision, and variety of definitions, internal colonialism is examined below as a theory, without any attempt to use a different terminology. The theory of internal colonialism is used to derive a hypothesis about ethnic activism. It is tested against empirical data for France, and it will be evident that although the theory of internal colonialism explains some aspects of the resurgence of ethnic activism, there is much that it does not explain. In the light of these limitations, the theory is revised and reinforced with the help of some theories about rebellion and political violence.

CHAPTER THREE

Internal Colonialism and Rising Expectations

In this chapter, we treat internal colonialism as a theory and test a hypothesis that derives from it. Although it is apparent that internal colonialism explains some of the ethnic activism of contemporary France, there is much that it does not explain. The second half of the chapter is a test of a complementary theoretical formulation, that of relative deprivation and rising expectations, to complement some of the deficiencies in the theory of internal colonialism.

1. INTERNAL COLONIALISM

The theory of internal colonialism was introduced in Chapter II; it holds that ethnic regions are preserved within industrial societies because they are held in a position of economic and political subordination by the central power, in a situation analogous to that of colonies of the classic type. Whatever the uncertainties and polemical misuses of the term, it is considered as providing a framework that merits examination for its capacity to explain the resurgence of ethnic activism in France.

According to the theory, ethnic discontent is the result of maintaining ethnic regions in a state of underdevelopment. This idea can be translated into a hypothesis, the "internal colonialism hypothesis," that *there will be a negative associating between measures of ethnic political militancy and measures of economic development.* Conversely, the higher the degree of economic development of an area, the lower will be the level of ethnic political militancy there.

Let us look first at the measures of the dependent variable used to test the hypothesis, those quantifying ethnic political militancy, and then the measures of the independent variable, economic development. Then the hypothesis can be tested by correlating the measures and the theory evaluated by comparing it with the evidence. Most of the measures are presented by department and ranked by region; the former are used for Pearson correlations when the data are available, and the latter are used for Spearman correlations when the data are ascertained only by region.

The easiest way to measure a political movement's strength is by the number of votes its candidates obtain in elections. Electoral measures are not enough, however, and some measure of nonelectorally expressed ethnic discontent should also be examined. There are data about ethnic candidates in presidential and legislative elections, and for the second there is evidence that demonstrations, bombings, terrorist attacks, or the lack thereof, can provide a measure of nonelectoral protest.

In the 1974 presidential election, federalist candidates ran for national office. These were Guy Héraud, candidate of the European Federalist party (Parti Fédéraliste Européen) and Claude Sebag, candidate of the European Federalist Movement (Mouvement Fédéraliste Européen). Though they identified themselves as federalists rather than specifically as spokesmen for the ethnic minorities, their candidacies were associated in the public eye with sympathy for ethnic activism. For instance, in one of Sebag's campaign speeches, he said,

In this country there are national minorities. These minorities, who have not been able to speak their languages for centuries, who have had to abandon their culture, must be able to express themselves. . . . To give back to the regions, and also to local groups, the ability to manage their affairs, to give them real power and make them living communities, is to restore democracy in France. *(Le Monde,* 28-29 April 1974)

Héraud, for his part, is the author of several books in which he explicitly takes the side of ethnic minorities. The ethnic aspects of these candidacies were emphasized also because on the eve of the election a third candidate, Robert Lafont, had been barred because his candidacy against *colonialisme intérieur* lacked four signatures on a petition. His supporters contended that the real reason was that the Constitutional Council was bent on "ethnocide" *(Le Monde,* 22 April 1974).

In all areas, the proportion of the vote Sebag and Héraud received was minuscule, but can be taken together as a measure of electoral support for ethnic activism in the different regions. The vote for Héraud is a clearer indicator of ethnic sentiment than that for Sebag. Héraud received 18,365 votes, of which 8,341 or 45.4 percent were cast in the ethnic regions, but the regions themselves represent only about 38 percent of the nation's votes. Sebag received 39,680, of which 10,575 or 26.7 percent were cast in the ethnic regions. The vote for Sebag is taken with the vote for Héraud, however, because it is possible that it took away from the vote for Héraud in the ethnic regions. The percentage of the vote for each is added together for brevity and to provide a composite measure of electorally expressed ethnic activism. They are shown in Table III.1.

TABLE III.1

Combined Percentage of Vote for Claude Sebag and
Guy Héraud in Presidential Election of 1974

Elsass	Bas-Rhin	.633
	Haut-Rhin	.552

Vlaanderen	Nord	.208
	Pas-de-Calais	.194
	Ille-et-Vilaine	.250
	Côtes-du-Nord	.278
	Finistère	.233
	Morbihan	.214
Euzkadi	Pyrénées Atlantiques	.581
Catalunya	Pyrénées Orientales	.302
Corsu	Corse	.148
Occitania	Haute-Vienne	.191
	Creuse	.017
	Corrèze	.174
	Allier	.157
	Puy-de-Dôme	.155
	Cantal	.164
	Haute-Loire	.193
	Lot	.224
	Aveyron	.187
	Tarn-et-Garonne	.267
	Tarn	.196
	Haute-Garonne	.239
	Gers	.239
	Hautes-Pyrénées	.271
	Ariège	.148
	Dordogne	.195
	Lot-et-Garonne	.236
	Lozère	.188
	Gard	.228
	Hérault	.197
	Aude	.165
	Drôme	.216
	Ardèche	.208
	Hautes-Alpes	.221
	Vaucluse	.306
	Alpes-de-Haute-Provence	.257

SOURCE: *Le Monde,* 7 May 1974.

An indirect measure of electorally expressed discontent is the proportion of ballots deposited blank or null *(blancs et nuls).* The latter is achieved by defacing the ballot in some way. In France, voting with a blank or defaced ballot is a common form of expressing opposition to the electoral system. Of course, the sentiment expressed need not necessarily be one of ethnic discontent, but it could be an indirect measure of its relative level. The blank and null ballots from an election in which ethnic candidates are not running should ideally be used. But such candidates ran in the legislative elections of 1973 and 1978, and in the presidential election of 1974. The percentage of blank and null ballots cast in the latter election is used as an instance, and is presented in Table III.2.[1]

TABLE III.2

Percentages of Blank and Null Ballots in
Presidential Election of 1972

Elsass	Bas-Rhin	1.5
	Haut-Rhin	1.7
Vlaanderen	Nord	0.3
	Pas-de-Calais	1.2
Breizh	Ille-et-Vilaine	0.9
	Côtes-du-Nord	0.6
	Finistère	0.5
	Morbihan	0.6
Euzkadi	Pyrénées Atlantiques	0.8
Catalunya	Pyrénées Orientales	1.0
Corsu	Corse	0.6
Occitania	Haute-Vienne	1.4
	Creuse	0.9
	Corrèze	0.8
	Allier	0.9
	Puy-de-Dôme	0.6
	Cantal	0.7

Haute-Loire	1.0
Lot	0.9
Aveyron	1.1
Tarn-et-Garonne	1.2
Tarn	1.2
Haute-Garonne	0.8
Gers	1.1
Hautes-Pyrénées	0.9
Ariège	0.9
Dordogne	1.1
Lot-et-Garonne	0.9
Lozère	0.9
Gard	0.9
Hérault	0.8
Aude	1.2
Drôme	0.9
Ardèche	0.9
Hautes-Alpes	1.1
Vaucluse	0.1
Alpes-de-Haute-Provence	1.1

SOURCE: *Le Monde*, 7 May 1974.

The presence or absence of bombings, demonstrations, and other manifestations is a measure of nonelectoral ethnic dissent. In Table III.3, the regions are ranked according to this level of protest in bombings, violent or nonviolent confrontations, demonstrations, or their lack. In this ranking Brittany is first, because waves of bombings have struck there since 1968, and confrontations between demonstrators and police have been frequent (see, e.g., *Le Monde*, 30 April 1968, 28 January 1969, 28 December 1973, and 28 July 1976).[2] Corsica ranks a very close second, for although it had little ethnically inspired violence prior to the 1970s, the level of bombings, armed attacks, and violent demonstrations has become quite high (*Le Monde*, 7 February, 28 April, 6 May, 1 September 1976; see also Desjardins, 1977). The Basques rank third, for though there have been no Basque bombings or attacks in France, there have periodically been large scale and occasionally violent demonstrations in 1965, 1971, and the summer of 1977 *(Le Monde,* 7 September 1965, 13 April 1966, 13 April 1971, 21-22 January 1974, 1 August 1977). Occitania ranks fourth, because it has cultural gatherings and university "summer schools" (actually political rallies and workshops) every year, but these are peaceful for the most part. Catalonia, Flanders, and Alsace are lowest in this measure, because their activity focuses on language, folklore, and art or orderly electoral activity. This ranking involves some subjectivity, because some might rank Brittany lower than Corsica or Occitania higher than the Basques. In any case, our criteria for making this estimation have been spelled out.

TABLE III.3

Rank-Order of France's Ethnic Regions,
by Level of Public Violence and Demonstrations

Elsass	6
Vlaanderen	6
Breizh	1
Euzkadi	3
Catalunya	6
Corsica	2
Occitania	4

Thus, to measure the internal colonialism hypothesis, three measures of the dependent variable are used: the percentage of votes received by Sebag and Héraud in the presidential election of 1974, the percentage of blank and null ballots in the same election, and the rank of the regions according to level of nonelectoral protest. Let us look now at the independent variable, measures of economic development.

Four measurements are used to measure the economic development in the departments of the ethnic regions of France. French census data are notoriously irregular in their compilation and comparability; in each case, the year used is as close as possible to the year of the dependent variable, 1974. Average annual income is an indicator of relative economic development, because people's in-

comes are affected by prosperity, and will tend to rise as the economy improves. Table III.4 shows the average annual income by
department for 1972. The percentage of the population engaged in
agriculture is a structural measure of economic development, in
that it is inversely proportional to the degree of modernization. It

TABLE III.4

Average Annual Income in Departments of
Ethnic Regions, 1972 (current francs)

Elsass	Bas-Rhin	18,197
	Haut-Rhin	18,379
Vlaanderen	Nord	18,427
	Pas-de-Calais	16,529
Breizh	Ille-et-Vilaine	16,935
	Côtes-du-Nord	15,906
	Finistère	16,806
	Morbihan	16,137
Euzkadi	Pyrénées Atlantiques	17,407
Catalunya	Pyrénées Orientales	15,197
Corsu	Corse	13,940
Occitania	Haute-Vienne	16,136
	Creuse	13,686
	Corrèze	15,446
	Allier	16,989
	Puy-de-Dôme	17,841
	Cantal	15,089
	Haute-Loire	15,278
	Lot	15,642
	Aveyron	14,574
	Tarn-et-Garonne	14,861
	Tarn	15,514
	Haute-Garonne	18,536
	Gers	14,373

Hautes-Pyrénées	15,489
Ariège	15,351
Dordogne	14,638
Lot-et-Garonne	15,159
Lozère	14,517
Gard	15,983
Hérault	17,367
Aude	16,790
Drôme	17,302
Ardèche	16,338
Hautes-Alpes	16,007
Vaucluse	16,885
Alpes-de-Haute-Provence	18,313

Ranks of regions

Elsass	1
Vlaanderen	2
Breizh	4
Euzkadi	3
Catalunya	6
Corsu	7
Occitania	5

SOURCE: INSEE, *Les Collections de l'INSEE M45.*
Paris: Imprimerie Nationale, 1972, pp. 74–75.

should correlate positively with indicators of ethnic activism, according to the internal colonialism hypothesis. These data are shown for 1975 in Table III.5. The third measure of economic development used is the "net regional product per capita," a rough translation of the *chiffre d'affaires des sociétés et entreprises, régime fiscale du bénéfice réelle.* As a per capita figure, it indicates the relative degree of business prosperity in the departments. These figures for 1972 are presented in Table III.6. Finally, an indicator of degree of urbanization is used, the percentage of the population living in urban areas. This indicator supplements the figure on agricultural population, because persons who leave the farm do not always move directly to the city. These data are shown for 1975 in Table III.7.

TABLE III.5

Percentage of Active Population Employed in
Agriculture in Departments of Ethnic Regions, 1975

Elsass	Bas-Rhin	5.3
	Haut-Rhin	4.2
Vlaanderen	Nord	3.9
	Pas-de-Calais	9.0
Breizh	Ille-et-Vilaine	20.6
	Côtes-du-Nord	28.0
	Finistère	21.9
	Morbihan	24.1
Euzkadi	Pyrénées Atlantiques	15.1
Catalunya	Pyrénées Orientales	15.5
Corsu	Corse	16.1[a]
Occitania	Haute-Vienne	13.8
	Creuse	38.5
	Corrèze	24.2
	Allier	14.8
	Puy-de-Dôme	11.6
	Cantal	31.8
	Haute-Loire	26.4
	Lot	30.5
	Aveyron	27.3
	Tarn-et-Garonne	30.0
	Tarn	15.9
	Haute-Garonne	7.3
	Gers	37.3
	Hautes-Pyrénées	14.9
	Ariège	17.6
	Dordogne	26.3
	Lot-et-Garonne	25.8
	Lozère	30.2
	Gard	12.6
	Hérault	12.5

Aude	22.8
Drôme	13.1
Ardèche	16.4
Hautes-Alpes	14.6
Vaucluse	15.7
Alpes-de-Haute-Provence	15.0

Ranks of regions

Elsass	7
Vlaanderen	6
Breizh	1
Euzkadi	5
Catalunya	4
Corsu	3
Occitania	2

SOURCE: INSEE, *Recensement général de la population de 1975. Fascicules départementaux.* Paris: Imprimerie Nationale, 1976.

a This figure was projected from 1962 and 1968 figures.

TABLE III.6

Net Regional Product Per Capita in
Departments of Ethnic Regions, 1972
(current francs)

Elsass	Bas-Rhin	29.1
	Haut-Rhin	24.8
Vlaanderen	Nord	28.8
	Pas-de-Calais	14.9
Breizh	Ille-et-Vilaine	10.9
	Côtes-du-Nord	14.7
	Finistère	18.0
	Morbihan	13.4
Euzkadi	Pyrénées Atlantiques	18.2
Catalunya	Pyrénées Orientales	14.2

Corsu	Corse	8.9
Occitania	Haute-Vienne	17.2
	Creuse	7.8
	Corrèze	12.9
	Allier	14.3
	Puy-de-Dôme	21.1
	Cantal	9.6
	Haute-Loire	12.9
	Lot	12.1
	Aveyron	13.2
	Tarn-et-Garonne	11.0
	Tarn	22.2
	Haute-Garonne	19.5
	Gers	12.3
	Hautes-Pyrénées	11.9
	Ariège	12.2
	Dordogne	11.1
	Lot-et-Garonne	17.6
	Lozère	9.4
	Gard	13.4
	Hérault	15.2
	Aude	12.4
	Drôme	19.3
	Ardèche	9.7
	Hautes-Alpes	13.2
	Vaucluse	20.8
	Alpes-de-Haute-Provence	12.2

Ranks of regions

Elsass	1
Vlaanderen	2
Breizh	5
Euzkadi	3
Catalunya	6
Corsu	7
Occitania	4

SOURCE: Ministère des Finances, *Statistiques et études financières, no. 325,* January 1976, pp. 9–12.

Annuaire statistique de la France, 1976 (résultats de 1974), INSEE, 1976, pp. 44–47.

TABLE III.7

Percentage of Population Living in Urban Areas in
Departments of Ethnic Regions, 1975

Elsass	Bas-Rhin	71.5
	Haut-Rhin	76.7
Vlaanderen	Nord	89.9
	Pas-de-Calais	80.9
Breizh	Ille-et-Vilaine	56.7
	Côtes-du-Nord	41.2
	Finistère	63.3
	Morbihan	48.9
Euzkadi	Pyrénées Atlantiques	67.3
Catalunya	Pyrénées Orientales	71.9
Corsu	Corse	44.7
Occitania	Haute-Vienne	61.1
	Creuse	22.1
	Corrèze	47.5
	Allier	59.5
	Puy-de-Dôme	51.4
	Cantal	33.8
	Haute-Loire	45.6
	Lot	33.4
	Aveyron	42.4
	Tarn-et-Garonne	47.6
	Tarn	64.8
	Haute-Garonne	76.9
	Gers	34.9
	Hautes-Pyrénées	58.5
	Ariège	46.2
	Dordogne	40.0
	Lot-et-Garonne	54.4
	Lozère	37.3

Gard	71.5
Hérault	77.5
Aude	53.8
Drôme	66.1
Ardèche	51.0
Hautes-Alpes	53.9
Vaucluse	75.7
Alpes-de-Haute-Provence	52.4

Ranks of regions

Elsass	2
Vlaanderen	1
Breizh	6
Euzkadi	4
Catalunya	3
Corsica	7
Occitania	5

SOURCE: INSEE, *Recensement général de la population de 1975. Population l   égale et statistiques communales complémentaires*. Paris:Imprimerie Nationale, 1976.

Table III.8 summarizes the correlations between the independent and dependent variables for the Sebag and Héraud vote, and the percentage of blank and null ballots. The correlation used is Pearson's *r*, because the data appear by department. For nonelectoral expressions, the correlation is Spearman's *r*, because the data are grouped by region. In calculating these correlations, each of the figures for each department ought to have been divided by the equivalent figure for France as a whole, because we are looking at relative prosperity in comparison to the whole nation. But because this would simply have meant dividing all the figures by the same denominator, it would have produced results no different from calculations using the data by department. The data are not divided by the equivalent figure for France in the tables, so that the reader may refer to the actual figures for each department.

One set of associations in Table III.8 is neither strong nor signifi-

cant, between the economic indicators and the percentage of blank
and null ballots cast in the presidential election of 1974. Though
this is often a measure of some kinds of political discontent in
France, it does not appear to be related to economic development
in the ethnic regions. The other dependent variables, however, do
show some strong correlations.

TABLE III.8

Correlations of Levels of Economic Prosperity with
Indicators of Ethnic Activism

	Average Annual Income 1972	Percent of Population in Agriculture 1975	Net Regional Product per Capita 1972	Percent of Population in Urban Areas 1975
Vote for Sebag and Heraud—1974	.48 p=.001	−.42 p=.005	.56 p=.001	.45 p=.003
Blank and Null Ballots—1974	−.01 n.s.	−.08 n.s.	.03 n.s.	.009 n.s.
Levels of Violence and Demonstrations	−.21 n.s.	.76 n.s.	−.49 n.s.	−.68 n.s.

   Between the economic indicators and the percentage of the vote
for Sebag and Héraud there are strong and significant associations:
.48 (p=.001) for average annual income in 1972, −.42 (p − .005)
for percentage of population in agriculture in 1975, .56 (p −.001)
for net regional product per capita in 1972, and .45 (p=.003) for
percentage of population in urban areas in 1975. The remarkable
thing about these figures is that the signs of the correlations are the
exact reverse of what would be expected from the internal colonialism hypothesis. If this hypothesis is true, levels of ethnic militancy
will be higher where the level of economic development is relatively lower, and activism less strong in the more prosperous
regions. The signs of the association between vote for ethnic candi-

dates and average annual income, net regional product per capita, and percentage of urban population should be negative, because these indicators rise as development increases. The association with percentage of the population in agriculture should be positive, because the higher this percentage the more underdeveloped the area is and the greater ethnic activism should be, according to the internal colonialism hypothesis. The signs of the correlations are in fact the opposite, and the strength and significance of the coefficients lead to a rejection of the hypothesis when the dependent variable is measured by votes for presidential candidates sympathetic to the ethnic cause.

None of the correlations of economic indicators with nonelectoral measures of ethnic discontent is significant. But the subjective ranking of the regions by levels of public violence and dramatic manifestations does show some strong associations. They cannot be considered significant, because the number of ranks is so small. The independent variable indicators of average annual income and net regional product per capita show associations that are small enough to be disregarded. The percentage of agricultural population and percentage of population in urban areas show quite strong correlations: .76 and −.68, respectively. Here the sign of the coefficients confirms the internal colonialism hypothesis. There should be more ethnic activism where more of the population is on the farm, because this indicates relative underdevelopment. Conversely, there should be a negative association between percentage of urban population and level of ethnic discontent, according to the hypothesis.

It appears that the internal colonialism hypothesis is to be rejected when ethnic activism is measured electorally, but it is to be accepted when ethnic activism is measured by levels of public violence and dramatic demonstrations. These are two kinds of political expression, the first associated with modernization because willingness to express oneself within the political channels available accompanies economic deelopment. The second is inversely related to modernization, because the more people feel excluded from the changes going on in France, and to the extent that they have been agricultural and nonurban, the more they will feel excluded from the political system as well, and vent their rage outside the established modes of political expression. This does not mean that nothing is changing in these heretofore undeveloped areas; in fact, it may be the rate at which their previously impoverished social structures are being disrupted that explains part of their ethnic activism.

Internal colonialism suggests that the uneven economic development of modern societies has led to preservation of ethnic regions. This would explain why Bretons, Basques, Occitans, and their minority brothers have not been assimilated into French society. But the theory does not explain the crucial question about ethnic resurgence in industrial societies all over the world today: *Why now?* Hechter acknowledges this shortcoming of the theory when he writes:

> The paradox of Celtic resurgence . . . is that it has occurred precisely during a period in which peripheral sectionalism has declined from its peak in 1924 and 1931: why do the nationalist parties suddenly gain strength in 1966? More fundamentally, why is there no apparent correlation between the measure of peripheral sectionalism and the level of support for the nationalist parties? (Hechter, 1975: 300)

In France, as we have seen, there is a correlation, but it is exactly the opposite of what we would expect.

It should not be surprising if the internal colonialism hypothesis and the thoery it derives from are only partially supported by the data we have examined. It is not the preservation of ethnic regions in a state of economic subordination alone that explains ethnic militancy. If this were the only factor at play, then the underdeveloped ethnic regions of all industrial societies would be in constant turmoil. This is palpably not the case. Some other approach must be used to explain why ethnicity is undergoing a rebirth as a political and social force at this time. This explanation may be afforded by the concept of relative deprivation, or a particular type, rising expectations.

2. RISING EXPECTATIONS

Studies of rebellion have made it clear that it is not so much abject oppression that produces militant dissent, but disparity between what people have and what they believe they can get. It is less absolute than relative deprivation, which may be the key to why ethnic militancy has reappeared now. Of course, the theory of internal colonialism implies relative deprivation of a kind, because the ethnic regions are unequal in relation to the rest of society. But relative deprivation in the sense in which it is used below relates to the changes that are taking place in France. Some change in the unequal status of France's ethnic minorities may explain the current revival.

Relative deprivation is a very old concept in the study of politics. Aristotle said that the commonest cause of revolution is "the desire of equality when men think that they are equal to others who have more than themselves" (Aristotle, 1943: 212). Tocqueville observed that, in the period preceding the French Revolution, the general economic and political circumstances had been improving. It was impossible to hold, then, that the Revolution was in any real sense a revolt against a "feudal" regime, regardless of the rhetoric of the rebels themselves. Instead, what prepared the way for the Revolution was discontent among the people who felt that the improvements, such as they were, were insufficient, and that when one demand was met, another appeared to be just as pressing. In his words,

> Patiently endured so long as it seemed beyond redress, a grievance comes to appear intolerable once the possibility of removing it crosses men's minds. For the mere fact that certain abuses have been remedied draws attention to the others and they appear more galling: people may suffer less but their sensibility is exacerbated. (Tocqueville, 1959: 177)

In this view of rebellion and revolution, the improvement of circumstances—political, economic, or otherwise—leads people to expect more than they have had. If these raised expectations are not satisfied, militant discontent will be the result.

The idea of rising expectations provoking revolutionary outbursts can fruitfully be applied to the problem of why ethnic activism has appeared at this time in French history. This is not to pretend that the scale of discontent or violence among France's ethnic groups is now anywhere near that of the Revolution of 1789. But the ethnic movements do represent an analogous development, because they question the political rules of the game as they have existed since the Revolution. They question it on two levels, first in that some reject the peaceful political process entirely and have resorted to terrorism and guerrilla activity. But even those who are so far still practicing peaceful tactics are questioning the very basis of the French political system. The keystone of Jacobinism is a unified, single French nation. Concepts of federalism or even ethnic diversity attack the very heart of the system. In short, despite the dissimilarities of the two situations, rising expectations may explain part of the recent ethnic resurgence, as they help to explain the Revolution.

Davies (1962) presents a refined and empirically testable version of the rising expectations theory of revolution. His thesis is that the revolutionary crisis occurs when a period of rising expectations and improving circumstances is followed by a sudden decline in "actual need fulfillment." This alteration produces a critical disparity between what people receive and what they expect. Miller (1977) indicates that there are some problems with the theory when tested with public opinion polls in the United States. If these data existed for France, we would examine them here, but there are not enough regularly compiled public opinion polls of ethnic minorities in France to do such a study. We must be content with a less sophisticated test of the rising expectations theory.

Gurr (1970) has written an elaborate set of hypotheses linking revolution and political violence to relative deprivation, an atti-

tude-set of which rising expectations are one type. He restates Tocqueville's thesis as one of his hypotheses:

> Marginal increases in value capabilities among deprived
> groups tend to increase the salience of the group's expecta-
> tions. (Gurr, 1970: 118)

When previously disadvantaged groups begin to experience improved conditions, their sense of injustice will increase rather than
decrease, because they will expect more than they had.

The rising expectations theory would hold that ethnic discontent
in France is the result of rapid improvement in economic circumstances in the ethnic regions. This interpretation is not contradictory to the theory of internal colonialism; it is complementary. An
area which has long been in a state of underdevelopment may also
by an area in which the rate of improvement is greatest. Although
the regions may, at any time, show a positive correlation between
levels of underdevelopment and ethnic militancy, in time there
may also be a positive correlation between improvement in their
economic circumstances and ethnic activism.

This analysis can be tested against current empirical data by
translating it into a hypothesis. This is the "rising expectations hypothesis": *there will be a positive association between measures of
ethnic political militancy and the rate of increase in measures of
economic development.* The higher the rate at which economic development occurs in an area, according to this, the greater will be
the ethnic militancy.

The dependent variable is the same for testing this hypothesis as
that used for the internal colonialism hypothesis, but without the
percentage of blank and null ballots (this indicator was shown not
to be relevant for ethnic activism). The vote for Sebag and Héraud
in 1974, and the rank-order of the regions by level of nonelectoral
protest were used. The independent variable is the rate of improvement of economic circumstances, measured by the rate of change
over time of the indicators used to test the internal colonialism
hypothesis. The four indicators are thus the average yearly percent-

age of increase in average annual income from 1963 to 1972, the average yearly percentage of decline in agricultural population from 1962 to 1975, the average yearly percentage of increase in net regional product per capita from 1963 to 1972, and the average yearly percentage of increase in urban population from 1962 to 1975. The intervals chosen span, as much as possible, the critical year 1968. The figures are presented in Tables III.9-12.

Table III.13 shows the correlations between the indicators of the independent and dependent variables for the rising expectations hypothesis. When the dependent variable is measured by the vote for Sebag and Héraud, two associations are neither strong nor significant: the average yearly increase in average annual income and the average yearly increase in the regional product per capita. The first of these is particularly interesting, because one would expect rising expectations to accompany increases in salary, which would in turn lead to greater ethnic discontent.

TABLE III.9

Rate of Increase in Average Annual Income in
Departments of Ethnic Regions, 1963–1972
(average percentage of increase per year)

Elsass	Bas-Rhin	13.6
	Haut-Rhin	13.1
Vlaanderen	Nord	11.9
	Pas-de-Calais	12.2
Breizh	Ille-et-Vilaine	13.0
	Côtes-du-Nord	13.1
	Finistère	13.2
	Morbihan	13.8
Euzkadi	Pyrénées Atlantiques	13.1
Catalunya	Pyrénées Orientales	12.3
Corsu	Corse	10.1

Occitania	Haute-Vienne	12.8
	Creuse	11.9
	Corrèze	11.6
	Allier	12.8
	Puy-de-Dôme	15.7
	Cantal	15.6
	Haute-Loire	14.0
	Lot	13.7
	Aveyron	12.2
	Tarn-et-Garonne	14.5
	Tarn	13.1
	Haute-Garonne	12.5
	Gers	14.0
	Hautes-Pyrénées	11.7
	Ariège	12.5
	Dordogne	13.1
	Lot-et-Garonne	12.2
	Lozère	11.6
	Gard	11.4
	Hérault	12.4
	Aude	14.7
	Drôme	12.4
	Ardèche	14.1
	Hautes-Alpes	10.2
	Vaucluse	11.6
	Alpes-de-Haute-Provence	10.5

Ranks of regions

Elsass	1
Vlaanderen	6
Breizh	2
Euzkadi	3
Catalunya	5
Corsu	7
Occitania	4

TABLE III.10

Rate of Decrease in Agricultural Population in
Departments of Ethnic Regions, 1962–1975
(average percentage of decrease per year)

Elsass	Bas-Rhin	0.8
	Haut-Rhin	0.5
Vlaanderen	Nord	0.2
	Pas-de-Calais	0.5
Breizh	Ille-et-Vilaine	1.5
	Côtes-du-Nord	1.7
	Finistère	1.3
	Morbihan	·1.7
Euzkadi	Pyrénées Atlantiques	1.2
Catalunya	Pyrénées Orientales	1.3
Corsu	Corse	1.2
Occitania	Haute-Vienne	1.4
	Creuse	1.6
	Corrèze	1.6
	Allier	1.2
	Puy-de-Dôme	1.1
	Cantal	1.6
	Haute-Loire	1.5
	Lot	1.6
	Aveyron	1.4
	Tarn-et-Garonne	1.3
	Tarn	1.3
	Haute-Garonne	1.0
	Gers	1.9
	Hautes-Pyrénées	1.3
	Ariège	1.7
	Dordogne	1.6
	Lot-et-Garonne	1.6

Lozère	1.7
Gard	0.8
Hérault	1.1
Aude	1.3
Drôme	1.0
Ardèche	1.5
Hautes-Alpes	1.5
Vaucluse	0.9
Alpes-de-Haute-Provence	1.2

Ranks of regions

Elsass	6
Vlaanderen	7
Breizh	1
Euzkadi	3
Catalunya	4
Corsu	5
Occitania	2

TABLE III.11

Rate of Increase in Net Regional Product Per Capita in
Departments of Ethnic Regions, 1963–1972
(current francs,
by average percentage of increase per year)

Elsass	Bas-Rhin	19.4
	Haut-Rhin	11.9
Vlaanderen	Nord	12.4
	Pas-de-Calais	22.0
Breizh	Ille-et-Vilaine	14.7
	Côtes-du-Nord	36.9
	Finistère	32.3
	Morbihan	32.6
Euzkadi	Pyrénées Atlantiques	16.2
Catalunya	Pyrénées Orientales	13.9

Corsu	Corse	98.8
Occitania	Haute-Vienne	23.0
	Creuse	22.2
	Corrèze	18.1
	Allier	18.3
	Puy-de-Dôme	18.9
	Cantal	26.9
	Haute-Loire	29.8
	Lot	27.3
	Aveyron	30.8
	Tarn-et-Garonne	24.8
	Tarn	22.2
	Haute-Garonne	20.3
	Gers	39.5
	Hautes-Pyrénées	27.8
	Ariège	26.5
	Dordogne	27.4
	Lot-et-Garonne	31.4
	Lozère	38.6
	Gard	14.6
	Hérault	0.1
	Aude	17.0
	Drôme	18.7
	Ardèche	18.0
	Hautes-Alpes	21.5
	Vaucluse	16.1
	Alpes-de-Haute-Provence	24.6

Ranks of regions

Elsass	6
Vlaanderen	4
Breizh	2
Euzkadi	5
Catalunya	7
Corsu	1
Occitania	3

TABLE III.12

Rate of Increase in Urban Population in Departments
of Ethnic Regions, 1962–1975
(average percentage of increase per year)

Elsass	Bas-Rhin	0.2
	Haut-Rhin	0.1
Vlaanderen	Nord	0.8
	Pas-de-Calais	0.8
Breizh	Ille-et-Vilaine	0.4
	Côtes-du-Nord	0.5
	Finistère	0.4
	Morbihan	0.3
Euzkadi	Pyrénées Atlantiques	0.4
Catalunya	Pyrénées Orientales	0.4
Corsu	Corse	0.2
Occitania	Haute-Vienne	0.6
	Creuse	0.4
	Corrèze	0.7
	Allier	0.5
	Puy-de-Dôme	0.2
	Cantal	0.5
	Haute-Loire	0.5
	Lot	0.4
	Aveyron	0.4
	Tarn-et-Garonne	0.3
	Tarn	0.4
	Haute-Garonne	0.3
	Gers	0.5
	Hautes-Pyrénées	0.3
	Ariège	0.5
	Dordogne	0.3
	Lot-et-Garonne	0.5

Lozère	0.5
Gard	0.1
Hérault	0.3
Aude	0.4
Drôme	0.4
Ardèche	0.6
Hautes-Alpes	0.5
Vaucluse	0.2
Alpes-de-Haute-Provence	0.4

Ranks of regions

Elsass	7
Vlaanderen	6
Breizh	3
Euzkadi	1
Catalunya	4
Corsu	5
Occitania	2

TABLE III.13

Correlations of rates of economic development with
indicators of ethnic activism

	Average Yearly Percent Increase in Income 1963–1972	Average Yearly Percent Decrease in Agricultural Population 1962–1975	Average Yearly Percent Increase in Net Regional Product per Capita 1963–1972	Average Yearly Percent Increase in Urban Population 1962–1975
Vote for Sebag and Heraud—1974	.0725 n.s.	−.37 p = .013	−.25 n.s.	−.34 p = .01
Levels of Violence and Demonstrations	.05 n.s.	.86 n.s.	.52 n.s.	.67 n.s.

The correlations that are strong and significant are the percentage of the vote for Sebag and Héraud with the average yearly percentage of decrease in agricultural population (-.37,p = .013), and the average yearly percentage of increase in urban population (-.34,p = .01). As with the internal colonialism hypothesis, however, the signs of these associations are exactly the opposite of what would be expected. If exodus from the countryside and migration to cities are signs of economic development, people's expectations should accordingly be raised and, according to the hypothesis, their ethnic militancy should increase. But exactly the opposite is shown by these associations. The more rapidly people are urbanizing, the less likely they are to vote for ethnic candidates. The slower the rate of urbanization, the greater the likelihood of electorally expressed ethnic discontent.

When we look at the rapidity of economic change as associated with nonelectoral measures, the rising expectations hypothesis tends to be confirmed. None of these associations is statistically significant, but for the average yearly percentage of decrease in agricultural population and average yearly percentage of increase in urban population, the correlations are high enough (.86 and .67, respectively) to indicate that they tend to support the rising expectations hypothesis. The sign of the coefficients is positive, as expected. If urbanization is occurring rapidly, people's expectations of its benefits should be raised and their ethnic discontent consequently increased.

As with the internal colonialism hypothesis, it appears that we are measuring two inversely related types of ethnic political expression, electoral and nonelectoral. The greater the rapidity of social change, the more likely people will be to express themselves outside legitimate political channels. When this change occurs at a more sober pace, people will be more likely to express themselves electorally, insofar as they evince ethnic discontent at all.

Instructive as these associations are, they suffer from the dependent variable being measured at only one point, whereas the independent variable is measured over time. A better picture of the relation between economic development and ethnic militancy would be provided by comparing how each of these factors changes over time. Unfortunately, the data for such a time-series study are sparse, and our results will not necessarily be conclusive. The most we can do here is present an addendum to the associations shown above.

In this test of the rising expectations hypothesis, the change in the percentage of votes received by the ethnic activist candidates in the legislative elections of 1973 and 1978 is the dependent variable. These figures are shown in Table III.14. There were eight candidates in the 1973 legislative elections and twelve in those of 1978, but in only six departments were there ethnic candidates in both elections. Four of these six are in Brittany, which means that the results of this test are not necessarily representative of the other regions.

TABLE III.14

Percentage of Votes Received by Ethnic Activist Candidates in
1973 and 1978 Legislative Elections

Department	1973	1978	Percentage of change	Rank
Haut-Rhin	4.5	3.3	−1.2	5
Ille-et-Vilaine	2.3	1.0	−1.3	6
Côtes-du-Nord	2.6	1.8	−0.8	4
Finistère	1.9	2.6	0.7	2
Morbihan	2.1	1.7	−0.4	3
Corsica	3.4	7.2	3.8	1

Source: *Le Monde*, 14 March 1978, 6 March 1973.

The independent variables are those used above: the rate of increase in average annual income from 1963 to 1972, the rate of decrease in agricultural population from 1962 to 1975, the rate of increase of business prosperity from 1963 to 1972, and the rate of increase in urban population from 1962 to 1975. Table III.15 summarizes the correlations of independent and dependent variables for this test. A Spearman rank-order correlation is used.

None of the correlations is statistically significant. The association between percentage do change in votes received and average annual income is .09, but when Corsica is removed, the association is .75. This figure is still not significant, because of the small number of cases, but still it is relatively high. The associations of rate of ·decline of agriculural population and rate of increase of urban population with the dependent variable are both low: .37 and −.26 respectively. The highest degree of correlation is shown between the change in the vote and the rate of increase in business prosperity, a correlation coefficient of .83. This is slightly below the coefficient required for significance at the .05 level with six cases, but it is still quite high.

TABLE III.15

Correlation of rates of increase in economic indicators with percentage of change in vote received by ethnic activist candidates

	Average Yearly Percent Increase in Income 1963–1972	Average Yearly Percent Decrease in Agricultural Population 1962–1975	Average Yearly Percent Increase in Net Regional Product per Capita 1963–1972	Average Yearly Percent Increase in Urban Population 1962–1975
Change in percentage of votes received	.09	.37	.83	−.26
by ethnic candidates, 1973–1978	n.s.	n.s.	n.s.	n.s.

These data provide weak support for the rising expectations hypothesis, in that without Corsica there is a high degree of association between the rate of change of votes for ethnic activists with the rate of increase in people's income, and with the rate of increase in business prosperity. Both associations are positive, meaning that as economic conditions are improving, people tend more to vote for ethnic candidates in legislative elections.

In conclusion, internal colonialism explains violent ethnic dissent, but is inversely related to electoral ethnic dissent. To the extent that ethnic regions are relatively underdeveloped, activists will tend to express their discontent in extra-electoral fashion; insofar as the regions are relatively developed, they will express themselves at the ballot box. To the degree that a region is excluded from the modernization that other parts of France are undergoing, the frustration will be that much greater, and a ballot box is a less satisfactory weapon for expressing frustration than a bomb. In ethnic regions that are relatively well off, insofar as there is any ethnic discontent at all, the discontented will vote for their representatives rather than resort to violence.

The rapidity of social change appears to have an even more complex relation to these measures of ethnic political militancy. There is apparently contradictory evidence with regard to the dependent variable as measured by the presidential vote for Sebag and Héraud, and for ethnic activist candidates in the legislative elections. The former showed an inverse relation, but the time series data showed strong but statistically insignificant positive associations. In view of the paucity and Breton bias of the latter data, the hypothesis must still be considered disconfirmed. One explanation of the apparent contradiction may lie in the different types of candidates, Sebag and Héraud were the first such candidates ever to run in a presidential election, and neither had a dynamic campaigning style. In outlying regions such as Corsica and Brittany, the response to such remote personages would undoubtedly be less warm than to local candidates of the sort who ran in the legislative elections. One other difference is the time that has elapsed since the presidential election and the latest legislative election in 1978. The militancy and violence of all ethnic dissent has increased greatly since then, and people may be more aware of the option of voting for this type of candidate than they were in the past.

There is an inverse relation between relative degrees of economic development and willingness to vote for presidential candidates who espouse ethnic causes. According to these data, then, the theory of internal colonialism clearly is incorrect. Internal colonialism does not explain the origins of ethnic differences, as the history of the ethnic regions makes clear, and it apparently does not explain levels of electorally expressed ethnic militancy in France. But it should not therefore be discarded.

There is clear confirmation of the relation between violent ethnic dissent and both internal colonial status and the present-day rapidity with which this internal colonial status is being erased. The relative deprivation of internal colonial status and the rising expectations resulting from the rapidity of social change are the explanatory factors for such outbursts and for their happening now. The relatively disadvantaged areas are also the ones that are catching up fastest, with the greatest consequent disruption of a stable—but backward—social structure. The discontent resulting from such rapid social change is called anomie, and anomie is used as an explanation of individual activists' motivation in Chapter IV. Internal colonial status is an explanation of how ethnic regions were preserved in otherwise modernizing states; it is the *end* of internal colonialism that explains violent ethnic dissent today.

In this chapter we have looked at the underlying causes of ethnic activism. The theories of internal colonialism and rising expectations explain part of why ethnic activism is undergoing a rebirth now. These theories do not explain all the present resurgence, and must be supplemented by the specifically French factors cited in Chapter II. A third set of explanations must be supplied, as for any social movement. In addition to unique historical causes, and causes common to all advanced pluralistic societies, ethnic movements are formed by and around a leadership. These leaders have social characteristics that help to explain why they have chosen this type of political activity.

CHAPTER FOUR

The Social Characteristics
of Ethnic Activists

In 1971, a newspaper reported the eloquently expressed feelings of a Breton activist:

> To live in this country is to suffer terribly, to feel that the people have no humanity any more. Life becomes routine. There is no more future. It is Sartre's absurdity. We are in a building being destroyed—alcoholism, depression, suicides. We must give back to the people the soul that has been robbed from them, along with the historical and cultural wealth of the Breton homeland. It's not just old stones that must be preserved—the Breton himself is a work of art in danger. (*Le Monde*, 3 August 1971)

No matter that the Bretons on behalf of whom the speaker is pleading have thus far paid scant heed. The emotions expressed are real and full of despair. To understand the social origins of these sentiments, we must look at the ethnic activists themselves, as a group.

The preceding chapters have shown that ethnic activism is, in part, a response to rapid social change. This is the point of view from which we examine the leadership, as a set of responses to a long-standing social order being swept away by the forces of modernization. Karl Mannheim provides a framework for this discussion. He discusses ideologies of the left and right, and of nationalism, as responses of the intelligentsia to changing social conditions:

> There are two courses of action which the unattached intellectuals have usually taken . . . first, what amounts to a largely voluntary affiliation with one of the various antagonistic classes; second, scrutiny of their own social moorings and the quest for the fulfillment of their mission as the predestined advocate of the intellectual interests of the whole. (Mannheim, 1962: 158)

The "whole" in this case refers to the whole of society, whether conceived of as an ethnic group or a nation. Being the advocate of the nation or national minority is an alternative to favoring one of the sides in the class struggle. The use of the term "unattached" with regard to the intelligentsia does not mean that they have no occupation; it means that they have no base in the proletariat or the bourgeoisie, and that their consciousness is therefore "free-floating." The intellectuals in question are not necessarily famous writers and professors in prestigious universities. They are highly educated, but they may be employed in modest occupations or may even be unemployed. Like Mannheim, Smith theorizes that nationalism is a kind of crisis of the intellectuals reacting to the rapid modernization of traditional society (Smith, 1971).

The critical question is whether or not modern ethnic activism is similar to the kind of nationalism Smith and Mannheim are talking about. This question can be tested empirically, and we will test three propositions against the results of a survey of leaders. These propositions should be true if the answer is in the affirmative.

If the leader of the ethnic activist groups are similar to the nationalists mentioned above, they should have a high proportion of intellectuals or highly educated persons among them. The first proposition about the leadership, then, is: *there will be a higher proportion of persons from intellectual occupations among the ethnic leadership than the proportion of these occupations among the general population.*

To the extent that ethnic activism derives from the responses of the intelligentsia to rapid change, the state of mind likely to give birth to ethnic consciousness is one of anomie. In its purest and original sense, anomie consists of a disparity between people's expectations and society's capacity to fulfill them. It is typically brought about by rapid social change (Durkheim, 1951: 252-255). On a macrosocial scale, it is brought about by fluctuations in such forces as business prosperity and by technological change. On a microsocial scale, it can result from social mobility (Lipset and Bendix, 1959: 63-64). Anomic dislocation as a result of social mobility has been identified as underlying ethnic identification. For instance, Frazier (1957) points out the self-conscious search for ethnic roots on the part of upward-mobile blacks in the United States. Emerson (1962: 54) says that leaders of anticolonialist movements are often people who have been "most dramatically shaken loose from their traditional institutions and patterns." This leads to the second proposition about ethnic activists: *there will be a higher rate of social mobility among the leaders than among the general population.*

An important aspect of Mannheim's formulation is that the activists scrutinize "their own social moorings," and undertake a "quest for the fulfillment of their mission" as leaders of the nation. In the case of the leaders under study, ethnic consciousness requires an active search for ethnic identity. The search for identity in general, among adolescents and young adults, has been elaborated by Erikson. Puberty presents adolescents with an internal revolution and the prospect of adult responsibilities in the future. Their central concern becomes integrating their self-conception with perceptions of them by others, and using previously acquired knowledge in the social world. With these formidable problems to solve, young people "are ever ready to install lasting idols and ideals as guardians of a final identity." It becomes important to establish in-groups and out-groups, and to make normally inconsequential items of dress or speech symbols for maintaining boundaries between the two. This often cruel practice is vital to avoid confusion regarding identity. It also requires stereotyping oneself and one's enemies, to reduce identity to dimensions simple enough to be easily grasped. Finally, it requires testing fidelity to the in-group.

Erikson argues that all these processes are accentuated by rapid modernization of the sort that is going on in the ethnic regions of France and elsewhere. The need for testing loyalties, he says,

> explains the appeal which simple and cruel totalitarian doctrines have on the minds of youth of such countries and classes as have lost or are losing their group identities (feudal, agrarian, tribal, national), and face world-wide industrialization, emancipation, and wider communication. (Erikson, 1961: 262)

Ethnic activism in France today does not include any totalitarian ideology—although in the interwar period it did—but it is simple enough, particularly in that it clearly delineates in-group and out-group for the purposes of self-stereotyping.

Berger (et al.) make a similar analysis on a social level. They talk of youth as a time of particularly acute searching for identity, a search made more desperate by modernization because modern social institutions provide no place for youth. This is why young people are at the same time the most estranged from themselves and those on "the most intensive quest for reliable identities" (Berger et al., 1974: 94). Both Erikson and Berger make it clear that the modernization of formerly stable—though possibly poor and "backward"—social orders will inspire a collective search for identity. For both psychological and institutional reasons, this search is most intensive among adolescents and young adults.

The third proposition is less precise than the first two. It consists essentially in the expectation that for ethnic activists, the cultural characteristics of their ethnicity will have been purposely acquired *after* childhood, as part of a general search for identity. Thus, for the leaders ethnicity is less a set of cultural data absorbed in childhood; ethnic language and other components of ethnic culture are sought out and acquired as a means of assuaging feelings of dislocation resulting from rapid social change and the experience of rapid social mobility. This proposition therefore holds that, for the leaders, ethnicity is achieved identity.

1. THE SURVEY

The source of information for testing these propositions is a survey of ethnic activists conducted during academic year 1974-1975 in France. The population studied were officials or organizations whose stated purpose was preservation of ethnic culture or achievement of some political autonomy or increased local power, or both, in the ethnic regions. The respondents also included poets, novelists, and singers who use their ethnic language as a vehicle.[1]

A questionnaire was developed to test these and other propositions about the ethnic activists (see Appendix II for facsimile). It was mailed to respondents with a return envelope to the University of Human Sciences in Strasbourg. In order to send the questionnaire to as many of these persons as possible, names and addresses were obtained from publications by or about ethnic activists and to political leaders mentioned in these publications. At the end of the questionnaire was a request for names and addresses of other respondents. Many answered this question, and questionnaires were sent to these persons. As the number of respondents increased, more and more of these names were repeated, which suggests that the total population identified is close to the total actual number of ethnic activists.

In all, 513 questionnaires were sent out and 264 responses received, some 52 percent. For a mailed survey, this is an extremely high response rate. Because no parameters of the population of leaders are known, however, no statistical tests can be performed to assess the representativeness of the sample comprising those who responded. There is probably some bias in favor of educated persons, because a written questionnaire requires a respondent to have some facility for expressing himself in writing. It might also be expected that persons with a history of clandestine ethnic activity would be reluctant to respond, yet among the responses were those sent by activists who had been arrested a number of times for illegal activity. Thus, although the sample cannot be mathematically assessed for bias, the comparatively high rate of response makes it possible to use it is an approximation of the ethnic leadership. The characteristics identified by the survey can therefore be used to test our three propositions.

To test the proposition regarding the leaders' social class, respondents were asked their occupation. In order to be able to test the occupational profile of the sample against that of the French population as a whole, these responses were grouped into the categories used by the French census bureau (INSEE). The categories are farmers *(agriculteurs exploitants* and *salariés agricoles)*, businessmen *(patrons de l'industrie et du commerce)*, professionals *(professionels libérales et cadres supérieurs,* white-collar workers *(cadres moyens et employeś)*, blue-collar workers *(ouvriers)*, service workers *(personnel de service)*, and others (artists, clergy, military, and police).[2] These categories are not quite refined enough to test the first proposition, because some teachers can be classed as professionals and some as white-collar workers.

As for the proposition about social mobility, the respondents were asked the occupation of their fathers, and the occupations of fathers and sons were grouped into three categories: nonmanual, manual, and farm. These three categories were used to permit comparisons between the sample and figures on the social mobility of the French population presented by Garnier and Hazelrigg (1974). They are broader than the categories used by the census bureau, but permit a clear picture of the comparative rates of social mobility.

With regard to the proposition about the purposive acquisition of ethnic culture, two sets of questions were asked. The first focused on ethnic language as a central aspect of ethnic culture, both because language is central to ethnicity as defined in this study, and because it is thought by the activists themselves to be a repository of their heritage. These questions asked what language the respondent's mother and father spoke at home, and at what age the respondent began to speak his ethnic language. The other set of questions was aimed at testing whether or not ethnic activity was embraced as part of a general search for identity. If they were started in late adolescence or early adulthood, it would confirm the suggestion that it solved part of the discomfort of being young in modern society. They were therefore asked at what age the respondent began his activity, and what the precise circumstances of his acquiring an ethnic consciousness were.

2. DATA AND DISCUSSION

Table IV.1 presents the data against which the first proposition is tested. This proposition suggested that a disproportionate percentage of persons from intellectual occupations would be among the leaders. There is a higher proportion of respondents among professionals and white-collar workers than in the population at large. Conversely, far fewer farmers and blue-collar workers are among the leadership, and no service workers at all. The proportion of businessmen is about the same. Insofar as professional and white-collar jobs require somewhat more education than the other occupations listed, the proposition seems to be supported.

An enumeration of the teachers in the sample sharpens this contention. Teachers variously fall into the category of white-collar or professional workers, depending on the level at which they are teaching. Of the 115 professionals in the sample, 74 are professors, and 24 of the 84 white-collar workers are teachers, mostly at the primary level. These two combined form 37 percent of the sample, compared to 3.8 percent of the population.[3] Overall, then, it is clear that the ethnic activists count persons in intellectual professions in numbers far out of proportion to the rest of the population, and the first proposition appears to be supported by the evidence. For a further discussion of these data, see Beer (1977).

TABLE IV.1

Occupational Distribution of Sample and
Total Actively Employed Population
(in percentages)

Occupations	Sample (N = 246)	Total actively employed (N = 20,398,000)[a]
Farmers	2.3	14.9
Businessmen	8.3	9.6
Professionals	43.7	4.9
White-collar	31.8	24.5
Blue-collar	3.0	37.8
Service	0.0	5.7
Others	10.9	2.8

[a] *Source:* INSEE, *Projet de loi de finances pour 1975:
Régions françaises—statistiques et indicateurs.*

These observations, of course, do not apply exclusively to ethnic activists. Militant organizations of the left and right show similar characteristics. Mannheim's argument is that all three of these types of militancy derive from the reactions of the intellectuals to modernization. Some figures on the occupational profile of a roughly contemporaneous militant party of the left, the Unified Socialist party, indicate a similar disproportion of educated occupational groups. Cayrol (1969) lists the percentages of members' occupations: farmers, 2.1; businessmen, 3.7; professionals, 22.5; white-collar workers, 36.2; blue-collar workers, 12.9. These percentages are extremely close to those of the ethnic activists, further confirming Mannheim's thesis and the first proposition.

The second proposition suggested that if the ethnic consciousness of the leaders stemmed from the personal experience of rapid social change, they would reflect higher social mobility than that of the French population. In order to make this comparison, two tables are necessary. Table IV.2 shows the rate of mobility among the

French population at large, and Tables IV.3 and IV.4 show the rate of mobility of the sample. The first illustrates father-to-son occupational change in France among males born 1918 and after who were still economically active in 1959 and 1964. The second table shows social mobility for the actively employed sample, and includes some who were born before 1918 and some who were not yet economically active in 1959 and 1964. The persons in this table, therefore, are not exactly congruent with those in Table IV.2: they are presented so that the occupational mobility of the whole sample can be shown. The personnel in Table IV.3 conform to the limits of Table IV.2.

The design of the tables is the same, comparing fathers' and sons' occupations in the nonmanual, manual, and farm categories. "Farm" workers in the social mobility categories are the same as

TABLE IV.2

Father-to-Son Occupational Status in France, Among Males Born
1918 and After, and Economically Active in 1959 and 1964

| | | Son's Occupation, 1964 | | | | |
		Nonmanual	Manual	Farm	Total	Distribution of origin
Father's Occupation	Nonmanual	$N =$ 1,017,400	510,800	36,000	1,564,200	
		$\% =$ 65.0	32.7	2.3	100.0	32.1
	Manual	$N =$ 456,600	1,155,400	28,000	1,640,000	
		$\% =$ 27.8	70.5	1.7	100.0	33.6
	Farm	$N =$ 289,000	612,600	774,600	1,676,000	
		$\% =$ 17.2	36.5	46.2	99.9	34.4
	Total	$N =$ 1,763,000	2,278,800	838,600	4,880,000	
		$\% =$ 36.1	46.7	17.2	100.0	

Source: Garnier and Hazelrigg (1974).

TABLE IV.3

Father-to-Son Occupational Status Change, for Sample
Born 1918 and After, and Before 1951

			Son's Occupation, 1975			
		Nonmanual	Manual	Farm	Total	Distribution of origin
Father's Occupation	Nonmanual	$N =$ 99	1	1	101	
		$\% =$ 98.2	0.9	0.9	100	53.2
	Manual	$N =$ 42	4	0	46	
		$\% =$ 91.3	8.7	0.0	100	24.2
	Farm	$N =$ 40	1	2	43	
		$\% =$ 93.0	2.3	4.6	100	22.6
	Total	$N =$ 181	6	3	190	
		$\% =$ 95.2	3.2	1.6	100	100.0

farm workers in the occupational distributions listed above. "Manual" workers correspond to blue-collar workers. All the other IN-SEE categories are classed as nonmanual.

To compare the sample of respondents to the French population, consider the marginal percentage totals of Tables IV.2 and IV.4. The fathers of sons in 1964 were distributed almost equally from the three categories in the population: 32.1 nonmanual, 33.6 manual, and 34.4 farm. The occupations of fathers in the sample were more heavily weighted toward nonmanual occupations, with 52.6 nonmanual, 23.3 manual, and 24.1 farm. Ethnic activists tend to come from relatively more prosperous origins than most Frenchmen. The marginal totals of sons' occupations in the sample reflect the high proportion of professionals and white-collar workers discussed above.

TABLE IV.4

Father-to-Son Occupational Status Change,
for Entire Actively Employed Sample

		Son's Occupation, 1975				
		Nonmanual	Manual	Farm	Total	Distribution of origin
Nonmanual	$N =$	148	2	1	151	
	$\% =$	98.0	1.3	0.7	100	52.6
Manual	$N =$	60	7	0	67	
	$\% =$	89.6	10.4	0.0	100	23.3
Farm	$N =$	63	2	4	69	
	$\% =$	91.3	2.9	5.8	100	24.1
Total	$N =$	271	11	5	190	
	$\% =$	94.4	3.8	1.7	100	100.0

(Father's Occupation)

Examining the percentages within the tables compares the rates of social mobility. Let us look at upward mobility first. Consider the sons whose fathers were farm workers: in the population, only 17.2 percent of them achieved nonmanual occupations, compared to 91.3 percent among the activists. The figures are similar for sons from nonmanual backgrounds: 27.8 percent of the sons in the population became nonmanual workers, whereas in the sample, 89.6 percent did so. In the population, the upward mobility of farm boys was largely to manual occupations, some 36.5 percent, but in the sample only 2.9 percent moved no higher than manual labor. The social change in France that has led to the rural exodus and the proletarianizing of the French peasantry led to a much greater change in life prospects for ethnic activists, who in one generation achieved much more upward mobility than did the rest of the rural population. The figures in Table IV.3 are not substantially different from those in Table IV.4, even with the more restricted portion of the respondents.

Anomie can also be the result of downward mobility, and to this extent the proposition is disconfirmed by comparing the tables. Of the sons of nonmanual origin in the population, 32.7 percent moved "downward" to manual occupations, and 2.3 percent to farm occupations. But in the sample there was practically no downward mobility at all of the sons from nonmanual backgrounds. Thus, there is a lower rate of downward mobility in the sample than in the population. To the extent that anomie resulting from social mobility explains the militancy of the ethnic activists, this has been exclusively upward mobility.

The third proposition holds that the ethnic activists would tend to have acquired their ethnic characteristics as part of a search for identity. The area of ethnic language is the first for testing this proposition. Tables IV.5 and IV.6 present the responses about languages spoken at home. The responses are broken down by ethnic region and by four categories of languages spoken at home by the respondent's mother and father: French only, French and ethnic language, French and other language, and ethnic language only. The third of these categories is not relevant for this discussion because the numbers are so few. They comprise only three families in which the mother or father spoke some European language in addition to French. There are three types of linguistic backgrounds, then: French only, bilingual, and ethnic-language-only households. The marginal totals show that proportions are about the same for mothers and fathers, so that it was not common, for instance, to have a bilingual mother and a French-only father.

Inspecting the marginal totals shows that about 42 percent of the leaders come from homes where parents spoke French only, about 35 percent from bilingual homes, and about 23 percent from homes where only the ethnic language was spoken. It is thus evident that only 58 percent of the leaders came from homes where the ethnic language was spoken at all, or, conversely, that 42 percent of the leaders never heard the ethnic language spoken at home.

The variations in the responses by region show some interesting extremes. Flanders has the heaviest concentration of French-only backgrounds, although the numbers are so small as to be hardly significant. On the other hand, Alsace shows the greatest proportion of ethnic-language-only households. It may be worth pointing out in passing that the strength of an ethnic movement has nothing to do with the extent to which the language is spoken by its leaders. Alsace and Flanders have two of the least vigorous movements, yet one has the highest and the other the lowest proportion of ethnic-language-only households.

Occitania has the highest concentration of bilingual households for activists. The similarity between Occitan and French makes this not so surprising. Brittany invites comment, for it has produced one of the most vigorous ethnic activist movements, which stresses language preservation very heavily. Yet more than half of the Breton activists come from homes where the language was not spoken, about 54 percent.

Table IV.7 shows the responses about the age at which the activists first learned their ethnic language. Overall, some 40 percent reported that they had "always" spoken the language. This is probably consistent with the reporting of bilingual or ethnic-language-only households in Tables IV.5 and IV.6. On the other hand, only 6.5 percent of the sample reported that they had never learned their ethnic language. Most of these came from Brittany, where the Gallo dialects, which are not related to Breton, are considered part of the Breton cultural identity. It is possible that some respondents who speak Gallo may have reported that they never learned their ethnic language, but meant Breton. In any case, it is evident that all but a very few respondents learned the language at some time in their lives. It is particularly striking that a majority of the respondents learned their ethnic language after childhood.

Inspecting the age categories reveals that most respondents learned their ethnic language during adolescence or early adulthood. The significance of this timing must be spelled out. On the one hand, it should not appear remarkable that people learn new languages in secondary school or undergraduate university educa-

TABLE IV.5

Languages Spoken by Respondents' Mothers at Home, by Region

		Total	Alsace	Flanders	Brittany	Basque Country	French Catalonia	Occitania
French only	N	118	3	7	57	6	2	43
	%	41.5	20.0	63.6	54.3	20.0	22.2	37.7
French and ethnic language	N	99	1	4	30	8	4	52
	%	34.9	6.7	28.6	28.6	26.7	44.4	45.6
French and other language	N	3	0	0	0	0	0	3
	%	1.1	0.0	0.0	0.0	0.0	0.0	2.6
Ethnic language only	N	64	11	0	18	16	3	16
	%	22.5	73.3	0.0	17.1	53.3	33.3	14.1
Total	N	284	15	11	105	30	9	114
	%	100.0	100.0	100.0	100.0	100.0	99.9	100.0

TABLE IV.6

Languages Spoken by Respondents' Fathers at Home, by Region

		Total	Alsace	Flanders	Brittany	Basque Country	French Catalonia	Occitania
French only	N	121	4	7	58	6	2	44
	%	42.0	26.7	63.6	54.7	20.0	22.2	37.6
French and ethnic language	N	96	1	4	28	8	5	50
	%	33.3	6.6	36.4	26.4	26.7	55.6	42.7
French and other language	N	4	0	0	0	0	0	4
	%	1.4	0.0	0.0	0.0	0.0	0.0	3.4
Ethnic language only	N	67	10	0	20	16	2	19
	%	23.3	66.7	0.0	18.9	53.3	22.2	16.3
Total	N	288	15	11	106	30	9	117
	%	100.0	100.0	100.0	100.0	100.0	100.0	100.0

TABLE IV.7

Age When Respondents Learned Ethnic Language, by Region

	Total		Alsace		Flanders		Brittany		Basque Country		French Catalonia		Occitania	
	N	%	N	%	N	%	N	%	N	%	N	%	N	%
Always spoke	118	40.1	12	63.2	2	18.2	27	25.2	20	25.2	6	66.7	51	43.6
1–9	13	4.4	1	5.3	0	0.0	0	0.0	2	6.5	1	11.1	9	7.7
10–19	80	27.4	4	21.1	2	18.2	36	33.6	5	16.1	1	11.1	32	27.4
20–29	53	18.1	0	0.0	6	54.5	24	22.4	3	9.7	1	11.1	19	16.2
30–39	8	2.6	0	0.0	1	9.1	5	4.7	0	0.0	0	0.0	2	1.7
40–49	2	0.6	0	0.0	0	0.0	1	0.9	0	0.0	0	0.0	1	0.9
50 and over	1	0.3	0	0.0	0	0.0	0	0.0	1	3.2	0	0.0	0	0.0
Never learned	19	6.5	2	10.4	0	0.0	14	13.2	0	0.0	0	0.0	3	2.5
Total	294	100.0	19	100.0	11	100.0	107	100.0	31	100.0	9	100.0	117	100.0

tion. But until the Deixonne Law was passed in 1951, it was not possible to obtain instruction in any of the ethnic languages in the entire school system. The Deixonne Law made it possible to choose an ethnic language as a third language for the baccalaureat, but did not provide instruction in these languages. Instruction had to be acquired elsewhere. It was not until 1976 that the French government decided to promote the teaching of ethnic languages. In short, the majority of ethnic activists who learned their languages in adolescence and young adulthood did so in spite of the hostility of the French educational system.

So far, the third proposition about the conscious acquisition of ethnicity by leaders appears to be supported, for the most part. The general definition of ethnicity includes language as a basic characteristic, but it is particularly important in France, where the stress on correctly spoken French approaches linguistic chauvinism. Many of the ethnic leaders come from homes where the language was not spoken at all, but only a few never learned their language. Fully 45 percent of the respondents learned their ethnic language in adolescence and young adulthood, in spite of the considerable hindrances they must have faced on the part of educational authorities. For Breton leaders the proportion was far higher, some 66 percent.

The proposition can also be tested by questions eliciting the age when the respondent began his activism and the precise circumstances of his acquiring an ethnic consciousness. Table IV.8 shows the data on the first question. The responses are not broken down by region, because there is very little variation, and because the small numbers in each cell undermine comparisons. Among the categories of responses, some activists replied that they had "always" been militant. These were put aside in a separate category, because they cannot be taken literally. There were also 37 nonresponses. Of those who did respond to the question, it is clear that most began their ethnic activism in adolescence or young adulthood, a total of 77.8 percent between the ages of 10 and 29.

This table, by itself, is not conclusive with regard to the third proposition. Most people begin their political activity, no matter what, at this time in their lives. But, taken with the information revealed in Tables IV.5, IV.6, and IV.7, it supports the expectation that ethnic activism serves as a means of dispelling doubts about identity in adolescence and young adulthood. Although it is true that most people begin political activity of any sort at these ages, this also may be in response to identity problems. As Erikson points out, simple and total ideologies are particularly appealing at this time of life because they provide clear definitions of in-group and out-group, and individual identity. In these cases, the search for identity has been solved by ethnic activism, but any other un-equivocal delineation of "us" and "them" could have done just as well.

TABLE IV.8

Age When Respondents Begin Ethnic Activity

Age	N	Percentage
"always militant"	6	2.3
1–9	1	0.4
10–19	106	41.2
20–29	94	36.6
30–39	31	12.1
40–49	15	5.8
50 and over	4	1.6
Total	257	100.0
Blank	37	

The last question aimed at testing whether ethnicity is achieved identity asked the circumstances that led to the respondent's gain-ing an awareness of his ethnic group. This question elicited quite varied responses, and some summarizing and categorizing were necessary. They varied from terse and uninformative phrases to long essays. Some responded with mere propaganda, such as, "I realized that Jacobin centralism tends to destroy different personalities in the hexagon" (the word "hexagon" is used to designate the geographic entity of France without conceding its political legitimacy.); "The awareness, in May 1940, that the French government had betrayed its citizens and had exploited the Bretons in its wars"; or "State nationalism of Europe, which led to the Second World War." These were intellectual justifications that may or may not be cogent, but they are useless for the purpose at hand.

Among the relevant responses were several recurrent themes, which could be separated into distinct categories. The eight categories revealed, and some examples, were:

1. *Contacts with other activists:* "I was contacted by activists from the Enbata movement"; "Deep regionalist feeling and meetings with activists"; "Meeting with other Occitans"; "Meeting other Occitanists during a stay in Marvejols in 1966".

2. *Reading the history, poetry, and literature of their ethnic group:* "Reading the first issue of the Basque newspaper *Enbata*"; "I found the newspaper *L'Avenir de la Bretagne* in a kiosque"; "I read some brochures and a book called *Complots pour une république Bretonne*"; "After relearning French history."

3. *Exile or emigration:* "The feeling of uprootedness during my studies in Paris"; "Exile in Champagne and then in Paris"; "Exile in Paris for my college education."

4. *Family upbringing:* "From my childhood"; "My conviction was formed progressively from infancy onward"; "By family training; my father was a militant"; "A feeling of injustice with regard to our language, ever since I was a child."

5. *Encouragement by teachers:* "A course in Occitan in the last year of school in Périgueux"; "I took courses in Gascon in the fourth and fifth grades in the institution where I did my secondary studies" [the institutions mentioned here must have been church-supported schools, because the state educational system did not teach minority languages]; "Courses taught by M. Robert Lafont at the University of Montpellier."

6. *Decolonization, Algeria, and the events of 1968:* "Discovery of

realities with the war in Algeria, in which I served as a draftee";
"The coup d'état of May 13, 1958, and the war in Algeria"; "Without a doubt, the problems of foreign decolonization."

7. *Learning the ethnic language:* "I always had the feeling that I
was missing something until I had the chance to learn the language
of my country"; "Through apprenticeship of the Breton language."

8. *Unpleasant experiences in school:* "The punishments I suffered
as a Breton-speaker in a French school"; "My differences with my
schoolmates"; "When I realized the consequences of the prohibition of Breton in school"; "At the age of 11, at the lycée of St.
Raphaël, the students and even the professors made fun of my
accent."

The frequencies of the responses in each category are reported in
Table IV.9. Not all the categories are very informative about the
sort of experiences that bring about awakening of an ethnic consciousness. "Contacts with other activists" does not tell why this
contact led to an ethnic awakening whereas the same exposure left
other people unaffected. Nor does it explain why presumable contact with other types of militants (left, right, religious, or whatever)

TABLE IV.9

Factors in the Formation of Ethnic Consciousness,
by Frequency of Responses

Category [a]	N	Percentage
Contacts with other activists	52	24.2
Reading history, literature, poetry	45	20.9
Exile or emigration	36	16.7
Family upbringing	35	16.3
Encouragement by professors	19	8.8
Decolonization, Algeria, 1968	12	5.6
Learning the ethnic language	8	3.7
Unpleasant experiences at school	8	3.7
Total	215	99.9

[a] Some respondents were counted more than once, because
they gave responses that fell into several categories.

did not move the respondents. "Reading history, literature, poetry" does not tell us what led the respondent to begin this reading, because the literature was always there. By themselves, then, the responses are not entirely clear, which is perhaps to be expected, being composed from brief responses to a mailed survey.

Comparisons, however, are instructive. Most outstanding, perhaps, is the small part played by unpleasant experiences in school. If ethnic awareness stemmed from the kind of stigmatization that accompanies racial discrimination, one would expect such reasons like this to be cited more frequently. Instead, it is the *least* cited of all the reasons. Almost as remarkable is the role played by *positive* experiences: contacts with other activists, reading, family upbringing, encouragement by professors, and learning the ethnic language together account for 74 percent of the responses. This indicates clearly that in spite of the movements' rhetoric about cultural genocide, internal colonialism, and the like, it was not so much suffering that led the militants to their ethnic awareness as supportive peers, professors, and family.

"Decolonization, Algeria, 1968" was set aside as a category of response contrasted to the propaganda statements, because it indicated that these dramatic shocks to the hegemony of the state had some influence on the activists' awareness. The experience of losing overseas territories in Indochina, West Africa, Algeria, and other parts of North Africa kept French society in turmoil from the late forties until 1962, and this was a time when many militants were going through their formative years. The relatively low priority of these factors among those cited, however, shows that although decolonization and the upheaval of 1968 proved ethnic militancy could have an effect, they were not responsible to any great extent for the appearance of ethnic consciousness itself.

These data appear to corroborate the third proposition. The "feeling of uprootedness," the "feeling that I was missing something until I had the chance to learn the language of my country" are clearly inspired by lack of clear identity. The remarkably small role played by unpleasant experiences at the hands of "them" indicates that the delineation between "us" and "them" was much more important in the minds of the ethnic activists than it was in the social milieu they were in. If ethnicity was something that had been imposed upon them by the French, it would have shown up in the responses. On the contrary, the militants tended to come to their awareness through positive and supportive acquaintances and kin. They embraced their ethnicity, rather than having it thrust upon them.

Of the three propositions, the third was the least precise, in that acquisition of an ethnic identity as a means of solving identity problems in youth is not the sort of process that can be unequivocally verified. The data presented do confirm this expectation, however. The fact that so many of the activists never heard the ethnic language spoken at home, that so many of them sought out and acquired their ethnic language in their adolescence and young adulthood in spite of official hostility, and that they cite positive rather than negative experiences as formative all tend to confirm that for the activists ethnic consciousness was often achieved in response to the needs of youth for a clear identity.

3. CONCLUSION

Ethnic activists are generally in occupations requiring intellectual preparation and have a great preponderance of teachers. This is true of ethnic activists in other countries as well. As a commentator on Basque, Breton, and Welsh activism writes,

> It is not the Basque or Breton peasants or the Welsh farmers who form the leadership of their respective national movements. Rather it is the young, the students, members of the professions and intellectuals who have become rootless, who recognize their condition and suddenly see that they have a weapon at hand. (Mayo, 1974: 8)

But why should such groups of people have come to feel so rootless? The reason becomes clearer when we understand the context of long-standing internal colonialism and the recent rapidity with which these regional differences are being wiped out. The intellectuals of today are no different from the intellectuals Mannheim had in mind, and, faced with the disintegration of a traditional social order—however provincial, poor, and "backward" it may have been—their choice has been with the parties of the left or right or the cause of the whole society from which they spring. Needless to say, most intellectuals in France have embraced the former, particularly parties of the left. For instance, a recent poll indicated that 70 percent of French teachers declared their intention to vote for the Communist-Socialist electoral coalition (*Le Monde,* 27 January 1978). But some evidently are opting for ethnic activism.

As if the crumbling of the social world around them were not enough, the activists' feelings of dislocation are accentuated by having experienced great transformations in their lives. The fixity of the French class system is far greater in myth than in reality, but the activists have experienced social mobility on a scale much larger than their compatriots had. When much of society is believed to be rooted in a class structure, the feeling of rootlessness can only be accentuated by being torn loose from one's original social ground.

Finally, rapid modernization and anomie were added to the already formidable problems of personal adjustment faced by the ethnic activists when they were adolescents and young adults. For a teen-ager the world is bewildering enough, and the search for a fixed group membership is often desperate. When society itself is drastically changing and one is leaving behind the familiar social world of one's family, desperation can turn to a search for a world that is simpler, cleaner, and calmer. Ecology, pacifism, evangelical religion, and some types of socialism can offer a vision of this kind of life, as does the fantasy of ethnic nations in pristine peace before the rude irruption of the modern world.

CHAPTER FIVE

Conclusion: The Genesis of
Ethnic Activism in Modern Societies

We have looked at the resurgence of ethnic activism in France from three points of view: the historical, the theoretical, and that of the leaders' social characteristics. These are complementary perspectives, and we will now attempt a synthesis. Let us consider first the general processes at work, because this chain of causation may explain the resurgence of ethnic activism in all industrial societies. Then we can examine how the specific circumstances of contemporary France exacerbated these already powerful forces. This will lead to an assessment of what the future is likely to promise for ethnic activism in France and elsewhere.

The starting point is the decline in importance of the nation-state in industrial society. This has been brought about by the appearance of supranational economic units, such as the European Economic Community, and supranational military units, such as the North Atlantic Treaty Organization. The centers of decision-making are less frequently in one's own national capitals and more often in remote places such as Brussels or Washington. Threats to nations are no longer from neighbors but from global blocs. Behind all this is the growth of a worldwide, interdependent economic system, which greatly reduces the gravity of national citizenship.

One consequence of the integration of industrial nations into a world system is the modernization of areas within these nations that had been until the present in a state of relative underdevelopment. This modernization was particularly painful and rapid in France, where the countryside had been stagnating under a policy of agricultural protectionism from the 1890s until de Gaulle. "Internal colonies," both ethnically specific and those which are not, are rapidly transformed, and mass migration from country to city, disruption of traditional value systems, of traditional ethnic and regional cultures are the result. This is particularly upsetting in ethnic regions that are unusually poor, and are sometimes viewed as invasion of a homeland by outside forces. This explains anti-modern and xenophobic interpretations of internal colonialism. Similar anomic feelings are doubtless experienced by people in regions that are not ethnically distinct, but they have no nostalgic ethnic vehicle for expressing them.

Those who are particularly articulate, the more educated of the population, react to these changes in several ways. As Mannheim points out, they tend either to go to the political right—meaning that they articulate some ideology of opposition to change and partisanship for the traditional ruling classes—or they can go to the left, embracing social change and attempting to shape its direction. In the recent past, French intellectuals have generally taken the second course, but in other periods, there has been a strong conservative tendency. A third option is to become a partisan of the whole group. This position can be either on the right or the left, because it contains the nostalgic element of the former and, particularly aided by the slogan of internal colonialism, the "popular" element of the latter.

These reactions are not simply intellectual reactions among the educated classes; they are reactions to radical transformations in their personal lives. Not only is their familiar social world being disrupted, they themselves often have undergone rapid social mobility. In an ethnic region where social mobility was difficult to achieve without emigrating, to become educated and consequently socially mobile may have had material benefits, but its psychic costs were high. The French ethnic activists are the counterparts of anticolonial Africans and Asians who have been, more often than not, educated at Oxford and the Sorbonne. Ethnic militancy is a self-conscious embrace of one's ethnic roots because of the role social mobility and education have had in tearing people away from them.

The search for identity becomes particularly desperate for adolescents and young adults. Not only is one's social world being transformed before one's eyes, not only is the experience of social mobility bewildering, but one is also faced with the problem of being a mature adult in such a tumultuous world. Young people from ethnically distinct origins have a ready-made in-group they can join, whose members are clearly distinct from nonmembers. In a sense, ethnic youths have an easier time of it because of the ready availability of a social identity. Non-ethnic youths are drawn to other types of in-group, such as those provided by pacifism, evangelical religion, socialism, and even terrorist cells. Ethnicity is therefore sought out as a solution to problems of identity raised by a world in turmoil.

This chain of events can be schematically depicted (see Figure V.1). The empirical context we have examined is that of France, but these processes are at work in all industrial societies that have indigenous, regionally based minorities. This framework can be empirically tested in other societies for verification and revision. In addition to these processes, some specifically French causes also explain the dimensions and nature of the contemporary ethnic renaissance.

This series of causes begins with the loss of oversease territories in Indochina and Algeria. These events demonstrated that the French state was highly vulnerable to a small group of dedicated nationalists, and in the latter case could be forced to give up territory that had been considered an integral part of France. The morrow of the Algeria war saw the beginning of the latest phase of

FIGURE V.1

The Genesis of Ethnic Activism in Modern Societies

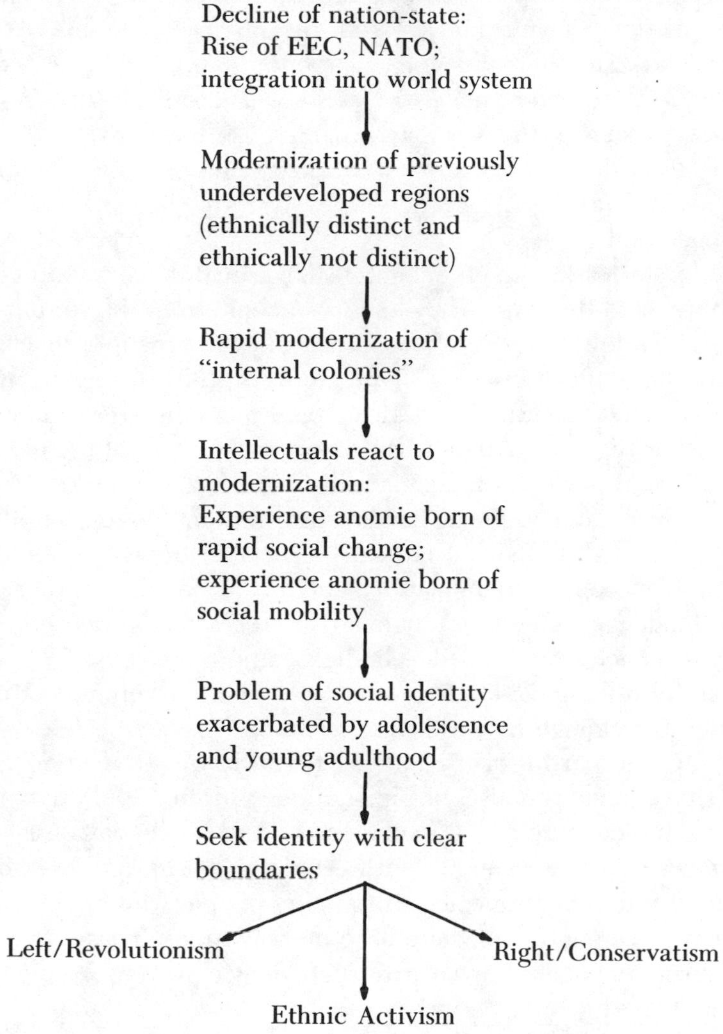

Decline of nation-state:
Rise of EEC, NATO;
integration into world system

↓

Modernization of previously
underdeveloped regions
(ethnically distinct and
ethnically not distinct)

↓

Rapid modernization of
"internal colonies"

↓

Intellectuals react to
modernization:
Experience anomie born of
rapid social change;
experience anomie born of
social mobility

↓

Problem of social identity
exacerbated by adolescence
and young adulthood

↓

Seek identity with clear
boundaries

Left/Revolutionism ←   → Right/Conservatism

↓

Ethnic Activism

ethnic activism, which was accelerated by another event that shook the state to its foundations, the Days of May in 1968.

Ethnic activism outside France also gave some powerful examples to follow. The postwar successes of Zionism and nationalist decolonization movements showed that it was possible to re-establish a state that had not existed for many centuries, or to establish a state where none had existed. Even the less successful movements, such as the Kurds and the Spanish Basques, showed the power of ethnic nationalism. If it worked outside France, it might work inside France. The French activist groups have also encouraged one another.

The forces leading to ethnic activism's rebirth have not all come from threats to the state. They have also come from the state itself, which in various ways has roused the hopes of people in ethnic regions about the possibility of regaining some power over their own affairs. The establishment of regional planning areas and commissions for regional economic development are two of these. Also, the discussion prior to the defeated referendum of 1969 raised the question of greater regional power. Government policy on ethnic languages has also changed radically. The Deixonne Law of 1951 was the first step in liberalization, but the recent declaration that ethnic languages would be taught in French schools was the most dramatic concession. And de Gaulle's famous outburst, "Vive le Québec Libre!" showed that he was sympathetic to ethnic activism abroad, even though he was less so at home.

Finally, the parties of the left, particularly the Unified Socialist Party, have made promises of regional devolution, should they gain power. The ideology of self-management and local control, known as *autogestion*, meshes easily with ethnic activism, and may have drawn off into non-ethnic activities many people who might otherwise have been active in the ethnic organizations. These promises may never be enacted, even if the left does gain power, but they have increased people's hopes.

We can also draw some conclusions about the ethnic movements with an eye to assessing their probable future course. The first is that ethnic activism is stronger now than ever in the past. It is also in a leftist political guise, in contrast to the conservative tendencies before World War II. The current position on the left, though, is probably more a reaction to the politics of the government in power in Paris. When Paris was republican, ethnic activism was royalist; when powerful Jacobinism and parties of the left appeared, ethnic activism tended to be fascist. If the left ever gains power, it is quite probable that the ethnic activist groups will revert to conservatism. The politically protean character of ethnic activism derives from the fact that ethnic groups cut across class lines, that ethnicity can be both nostalgic and antimodern, and can pose as defender of the people against "foreign" exploiters.

In many ways, the ethnic leaders are more like the leaders of other militant political groups than they are like their own constituency. Breton activists have predominantly the same social origins, experiences, and outlook as activists from Alsace—or militants from the Unified Socialist Party, for that matter. They are similar apparently because political activists, no matter what their ideology, tend to come from educated classes that are reacting in some way to social change. In this sense, there is certainly a close similarity between the present-day ethnic activists in industrial societies and the nationalists of nineteenth-century Europe and the contemporary Third World. All are conscious of their ethnicity because of the influence of modernization on their societies and on their own lives.

Internal colonialism, despite the many polemical and sloppy uses of the term, can be considered as a theory to explain ethnic activism in industrial society. As such, it explains much of the violent ethnic dissent, but must be revised to fit electorally expressed ethnic resentment. The theory of relative deprivation in the particular form of rising expectations supplements some weaknesses of the theory of internal colonialism. The speed with which former internal colonial status is being wiped out also helps to explain why violent ethnic dissent is occurring now. When such change occurs at an orderly pace, ethnic militancy is expressed through the ballot box rather than with bombs.

What is the probable course of ethnic activism in industrial so-

cieties in general? Much depends on where political soil is fertile
for affiliations along ethnic lines. This in turn depends on what
other modes of political aggregation are present and how firmly
entrenched they are. One of the reasons ethnic activism is relatively weak in France is the persistence of political affiliation by
class. Not that different political parties have followings exclusively
from particular classes; rather, the terms of discourse in politics are
expressed as class antagonism.

Ethnic activism has found much more support in societies where
ethnicity has always been as strong as or stronger than other principles of political alignment, such as Belgium or Canada. If France's
political vocabulary goes beyond that of class conflict, ethnicity
might well become a new mode of political affiliation, as Glazer
and Moynihan argue that it has in the United States. This can only
happen if long-standing regional inequalities and gross inequalities
of class that persist in French society are also alleviated. The former is already happening, but it is not certain when or how the
latter will be accomplished. If class inequalities can somehow be
reduced, it is quite likely that new principles of social and political
affiliation will take their place, and one of these is bound to be
ethnicity. Ethnic activism in France could become much more of a
force than it is today.

Appendix I

In this Appendix is a listing of all the ethnic activist organizations discovered in the survey described in Chapter IV. The addresses of the organizations are provided where they are known. They are also characterized by their conventional political orientation when it was known—extreme left, left, conservative. They are also described as cultural, regionalist, federalist, autonomist, or separatist, according to the type of activity they carry on or what they view as the measures necessary for their ethnic regions. When ascertained, their founding dates are added as well. Not all these groups are still in existence, some having vanished soon after their foundation, and some losing their memberships to groups founded subsequently. Publications are listed following organizations, and are italicized; most are publications of organizations, but some are independent. Many of the organizations are listed in Jaubert (1974).

ALSACE

Cercle René Schickele	cultural	1968
11, Place de Bordeaux		
67 Strasbourg		

Comité Libération Mulhouse	extreme left	1973
Comité Libération Strasbourg	extreme left	1973
Conseil des Ecrivains d'Alsace 1, Quai Charles Frey 67 Strasbourg	cultural	1971
Front Culturel Alsacien	far left autonomist	1974
Mouvement Régionaliste d'Alsace Lorraine Movement Féderaliste Européen Région-Alsace	conservative regionalist federalist	1970
Musauer Wäckes	cultural	1972
Parti Fédéraliste d'Alsace- Lorraine BP 192 Meinau 67 Strasbourg	federalist	1972

ALSACE (publications)

Cahiers du Cercle René Schickele
publication of Cercle RenéSchickele

Elsa
publication of Mouvement Régionaliste
d'Alsace-Lorraine

Klapperstei 68 1 Blvd. Président Roosevelt 68 Mulhouse	left cultural	1972
Libération Alsace publication of Comité Libération Strasbourg	extreme left	1973

Paysans d'Alsace 21 rue de l'Eglise 68 Artzenheim	extreme left	1973

Rot Un Wiss
publication of Parti Fédéraliste
d'Alsace-Lorraine

Uss'm Follik	left cultural	1971

La Voix d'Alsace-Lorraine 25 rue de la Fidélité 68 Mulhouse	federalist	1953

FLANDERS

Cercle "Les Amis de la Flandre Française"	cultural	

Heckeschreeuwen Eeckestraete 42 59 Steenvorde	left cultural	

Michiel de Swaën Kring BP 9 59 Malo-Dunkerque	cultural	1972

Section Fédéraliste du Pays-Bas Français	federalist	

FLANDERS (Publications)

Le Courrier Lillois publication of Michiel de Swaën Kring BP 1080 59 Lille	cultural	1971

La Nouvelle Flandre publication of Section Fédéraliste du Pays-Bas Français	federalist	1970

BRITTANY

Adsav 1532 10, rue du Champ de Foire 22 Mur de Bretagne	autonomist	1971
Al Leur Nevez 19, rue du Front 29 Quimper	cultural	
Ar Falz Straed Kan Ar Gwez 29 Plourin-Montroulez	cultural	1945
Ar Skol Dre Lizer (Ecole par Correspondance)	cultural	1945
Association des Chanteurs Bretons Fay de Bretagne 44 Blain		
Association pour le Développement Economique de la Bretagne		
Association des Professeurs de Breton des Ecoles Laïques	cultural	
Association des Professeurs de Breton de l'Enseignement Libre	cultural	
Beleien Vreizh (Prêtres de Bretagne)	cultural	
Bleun-Brug 5 rue Francis Jammes 29 Brest	cultural	1948

Bodadeg Ar Sonerion   cultural   1946
(Association des Sonneurs)

Breizh Yaouank
(Jeune Bretagne)
BP 61 Rennes

Bretagne Vivante   cultural

Brudan Ha Skignan
(Agence Bretonne d'Information)
30 Place des Lices
35 Rennes

Cercle Nantais de Culture Celtique   cultural

Gorsedd   cultural   1966
(Collège des Druides, Bardes
et Ovates de Bretagne)
Kerig Ar Vro
49 La Chapelle sur Erdre

Comité d'Action pour la   left   1969
Langue Bretonne   cultural

Comité Européen de Défense du   federalist   1969
Peuple Breton

Comité de Liaison de l'Action   left   1967
Régionale et Progessiste de
Bretagne

Comités d'Action Bretons   extreme left   1972
26 Allée Bergson
35 Rennes

Comité d'Action pour un Statut de   cultural
la Langue Bretonne

Comité d'Etudes et de Liaison des Intérêts Bretons 7 Place de Bretagne 35 Rennes	regionalist	1950
Confédération des Sociétés Culturelles, Artistiques et Folkloriques de Bretagne (Kendalc'h) 4 Allée des Ormeaux 45 La Baule	cultural	1950
Dastum (Magnétothèque Nationale Bretonne)		
Eglise Catholique Orthodoxe de Bretagne		
Emgleio Breiz BP 17 29 Brest	cultural	
Front de Libération de la Bretagne	separatist	1967
Groupe d'Etudes Politiques Bretonnes et Internationales	extreme left	1971
Jeunesse Etudiante Bretonne	autonomist	1963
Jeunesses Progressistes de Bretagne BP 221 29 Brest	cultural	
Kamp Etrekeliek Ar Vrezhonegerion (Camp Breton Ouvert à la Jeunesse des Pays Celtiques)	cultural	1948

Kelc'h Sevendruel Gwened 2 rue des Tribuneaux 56 Vannes	cultural	1973
Kuzul Ar Brezhonek (Conseil de la Langue Bretonne) 28 rue des Trois Frères LeGoff 22 St. Brieuc	cultural	
Movement pour l'Organisation de la Bretagne	autonomist	1957
Parti Communiste Breton (Strollad Komunour Breizh)	left autonomist	1971
Les Rotatives de la Colère Bretonne BP 54 56 Enoriant	extreme left autonomist	1973
Stourm Breizh (Résistance Bretonne) 37 rue Vasselot 35 Rennes	extreme left autonomist	1974
Strollad Ar Vro (Le Parti du Pays) 7 rue des Chapeliers 22 Lannion	autonomist	1973
Survivre en Bretagne BP 54 56 Enoriant	ecological	1972
Union Démocratique Bretonne BP 304 29 Brest	left autonomist	1964

BRITTANY (Publications)

Al Liam publication of Kuzul Ar Brezhonek	cultural	
An Tribann publication of Gorsedd	cultural	1952
Ar Falz publication of Ar Falz	cultural	
Ar Gevenidenn (Revue des Jeunes en Langue Bretonne)	cultural	
Ar Morzhol publication of Jeunesses Progressistes de Bretagne	cultural	
Ar Soner publication of Bodadeg Ar Sonerion	cultural	1946
l'Avenir de la Bretagne publication of Strollad Ar Vro	autonomist	
Bleun-Brug publication of Bleun-Brug	cultural	
Breiz publication of Confédération des Sociétés Culturelles, Artistiques et Folkloriques de Bretagne	cultural	
Bretagne Information et Action publication of Comité d'Etudes et de Liaison des Intérêts Bretons	regionalist	

Bretagne Magazine	cultural	1968
Bretagne Révolutionnaire publication of Parti Communiste Breton	autonomist	
Combat Breton 18, rue Saint Gueno 22 St Brieuc publication of Strollad Ar Vro	autonomist	
Douar Breiz publication of Adsav 1532	autonomist	
L'Etudiant Breton BP 7 29 Brest publication of Jeunesse Etudiante Bretonne	autonomist	
Evi Har Brezoneg (Pour la Langue Bretonne) Beg-Leguer 22 Lannion	left cultural	1973
Hor Yezh (Revue de Linguistique et d'Etudes en Langue Bretonne)	cultural	
Imburc'h (Revue d'Etudes en Langue Bretonne)	cultural	
La Peuple Breton publication of the Union Démocratique Bretonne	left autonomist	
Preder (Revue d'Etudes en Langue Bretonne)	cultural	

Sav Breizh	left cultural	1969
Skol (Revue Pédagogique en Langue Bretonne) 16, rue Berlioz 22 St Brieuc	cultural	
Skol Vreiz publication of Ar Falz	cultural	
Skrid (Revue Littéraire en Langue Bretonne) Section de Celtique Université de Haute-Bretagne 35 Rennes	cultural	
Taolenn (Bulletin d'Information et de Critique Bibliographiques, Bretonnes et Internationales) Ker Arvor 44 Loroux	cultural	

FRENCH BASQUE COUNTRY

Enbata	separatist	1963
Eskualzaleen Biltzarra (Association des Amis de la Langue Basque)	cultural	
Euskal Elkargoa 16 rue de la République 64 St Jean de Luz	cultural	

Euskal Gogoa   cultural
21 Bourgneuf
64 Bayonne

Ikas   cultural
15 rue du Port Neuf
64 Bayonne
Mende Berri   cultural
32 rue Bourgneuf
64 Bayonne

Mouvement Fédéraliste Européen-   federalist
Section Basque

Parti Socialiste Basque   left   1974
BP 192
64 Bayonne

Seaska   cultural   1969

FRENCH BASQUE COUNTRY (Publications)

Elgar   federalist
publication of Mouvement Fédéraliste
Européen-Section Basque

Enbata   separatist
publication of Enbata
14 rue des Cordeliers
64 Bayonne

Euskaldunak   left
publication of Parti Socialiste
Basque

FRENCH CATALONIA

Acció Regionalista Catalana	federalist	1969
Comité Roussillonais d'Etudes et d'Animation 16 Carrer Petit de la Real 66 Perpignan	extreme left	1970
Esquerra Catalana dels Traballadores 10 Carrer Foy 66 Perpignan	extreme left	1972
Gauche Ouvrière et Paysanne Roussillonaise Grup Guilhem de Cabestany	extreme left cultural	1973

FRENCH BASQUE COUNTRY (Publication)

La Falç publication of Comité Roussillonais d'Etudes et d'Animation	extreme left

OCCITANIA

Action Poésie-Occitan 4 rue Alexandre Bertereau 92 Neuilly	left cultural	1971
Les Amis de la Langue d'Oc à Paris 95 Blvd Raspail 75 Paris 6e	cultural	
Aparamen 2 Chemin de la Baume Loubière 13 Marseille	cultural	1970

Association per la Defensa dans Arts Occitans 102A rue F. Perrin 87 Limoges	left cultural	
Atelier Occitan Peire d'Auvernha 3 Cité Montplain 15 St. Flour	left autonomist	1972
Centre Bordelais de Documentation Occitane 25 bis rue Louis Liard 33 Bordeaux	cultural	
Centre Culturel Occitan 4 bis rue des Bernardins 13 Aix	left cultural	
Centre Culturel Occitan de l'Etang de Berre 11 rue de la Fraternité 15 Martigues	left regionalist cultural	1973
Centre Dramatique Occitan 34 rue St Cyprien 83 Toulon	cultural	1970
Centre International de Documentation Occitane		
Centre Régional d'Etudes Occitanes 5 Traverse Cas 13 Marseille	left autonomist	1970
Cercle Limousin d'Etudes Occitanes BP 265 87 Limoges	cultural regionalist	1971

Cercle Populaire de Culture Occitane 26 Blvd des Dames 13 Marseille	cultural	1973
Cinéma Occitan 99 rue Didiot 75 Paris	left cultural	1972
Comitat Rocabrunenc d'Estudis Occitans Le Saint Eloi 83 Roquebrune	extreme left cultural	1973
Comité Occitan d'Unité Populaire	extreme left	1972
Fédération Anarchiste-Communiste d'Occitanie 33 rue des Vignolles 75 Paris	extreme left	1969
Front Occitan 43110 Aurec	extreme left	1973
Institut d'Etudes Occitanes 11 bis rue de la Concorde 31 Toulouse	cultural	1945
Mouvement Populaire Occitan	autonomist	1974
Parti Nationaliste Occitan BP 232 87 Limoges	conservative	1959
Parti Socialiste Occitan	left	
Per Noste Avenue des Pyrénées 64 Orthez	cultural	1966

Teatra de la Carrera   extreme left   1970
rue des Camisards   cultural
30 Le Grau du Roi

Vida Nostra   left   1966
BP 178   regionalist
31 Toulouse

OCCITANIA (Publications)

L'Astrado Prouvençalo   cultural
2 rue Vincent Allègre
83 Toulon

La Clau Lemosina
publication of Cercle Limousin
d'Etudes Occitanes

L'Estanh de Berra
publication of Centre Culturel
Occitan de l'Etang de Berre

Fors-Revista Bearnesa d'Accion   left   1971
Occitana   regionalist
13 rue Abbé Bremont   cultural
64 Pau

Libération Occitanie   extreme left   1973
3 Blvd Arcole
31 Toulouse

Lu Lugar   conservative
publication of Parti Nationaliste
Occitan

Lutte Occitane   extreme left   1971
BP 2132
34 Montpellier

Novelum 24600 Riberac publication of the Périgord Section of the Institut d'Etudes Occitanes	cultural	1969
Oc 11 rue Croix Baragon 31 Toulouse	cultural	1923
Occitania Nova publication of Institut d'Etudes Occitanes	cultural	1969
Occitanie Libertaire publication of the Federation Anarchiste- Communiste d'Occitanie		
Poble d'Oc BP 131 34 Montpellier	conservative	
Réalité Occitane et *Christianisme*		1966
Lo Reveilh d'Oc 31130 Balma	cultural	1972
Le Rictus Occitan 18-20 rue Gatien Arnoult 31 Toulouse	left cultural	1973
Vida Nostra publication of Vida Nostra		

Appendix II

UNIVERSITE DES SCIENCES HUMAINES DE STRASBOURG
FACULTE DES SCIENCES HISTORIQUES
INSTITUT D'HISTOIRE ECONOMIQUE ET SOCIALE

Groupe de Recherches sur les Sociétés Contemporaines

M. BEER
16, rue Frédéric
67100 STRASBOURG

QUESTIONNAIRE

1 - NOM : ....   2 - Date de naissance : ....

Prénoms : ....   2a - Domicile habituel : ....

3 - Lieu de naissance : ....

3a- Si vous êtes né en ...., avez-vous vécu toute votre vie en
.... ?

4 - Quel est votre métier (ou, si vous êtes retraité, quel était-il) ?
....

4a- Quel était le métier de votre père ?
....

5 - Quelle langue parlait votre mère à la maison ? ....

5a- Quelle langue parlait votre père à la maison ? ....

5b- Si la famille était francophone à quel âge avez-vous commencé à apprendre la
langue de votre minorité ? ....

6 - Quelles sont vos activités de militant ? ....

6a- A quel âge avez-vous commencé votre activité de militant ? ....

6b- Quelles ont été les circonstances précises de votre prise de conscience ?
....

6c- Avez-vous milité dans un groupe ou un parti politique non-nationalitaire (hexagonal) ? ....

6d- Lequel ? Ou si vous l'avez quitté, pourquoi et quand ? ....

6e- Si vous y êtes toujours, pourquoi ? ....

7 - Quant à la religion, vous considérez-vous pratiquant, non-pratiquant ou athée ?
....

7a- Catholique
Protestant
Autre : ....

8 - Avez-vous conservé des archives concernant votre action individuelle ou celles
d'organisations auxquelles vous avez appartenu ? ....

9 - Dans quelles conditions accepteriez-vous de communiquer ces documents aux
chercheurs ? ....

10 - Connaissez-vous d'autres militants régionalistes ? Pouvez-vous nous donner
leurs adresses ? ....

133

Notes

INTRODUCTION

1. The United States is not included in this list because of an important difference between ethnicity there and elsewhere. In the United States, with the exception of Hawaiians, Eskimos, and American Indians, ethnic groups are urbanized national-origin groups. Elsewhere in the world they are, for the most part, regionally based, indigenous groups. In the United States they are largely assimilated, regardless of the symbolic importance they may place on their authentic or synthetic distinctiveness. Elsewhere in the world, ethnic regions are for the most part ancient, and ethnic languages are still spoken in everyday life. In short, the theories that apply to ethnicity outside the United States are not necessarily applicable to ethnicity in the United States.

2. "Ethnic group" is, in the linguistic and cultural senses, the modern counterpart of the word "nation," as used by nineteenth-century thinkers such as Fichte, and by Marxists such as Stalin. Carleton Hayes uses "nationality" in the same sense. Because nation and nationality are so easily confused with statehood and state affiliation, these terms are used less and less today. The legacy of confusion left by earlier terminologies, however, is immense.

3. Connor's term, "ethnonationalism," is not used because it implies the exclusion of ethnic regionalism (Connor, 1973).

CHAPTER I

1. In 1539, the Edict of Villers-Cotterêts declared French the only official language of the kingdom; that the edict had become necessary is an indication of how much competition French had from the languages of the conquered peoples. These tongues were, and are still, considered by many Frenchmen to be merely local dialects rather than languages in their own right. What they are called, *patois* or national languages, depends on one's political perspective.

2. The very severity of this subjugation may have produced the beginnings of solidarity among provinces that had been politically separate. One historian argues that, "Everything leads to the conclusion that Occitania degenerated under the old regime. . . . But at the same time the period showed—perhaps for the first time in history—the birth of consciousness at the social level. At the time of its greatest glory, Occitania had never had such an awareness of itself on the collective level (Espieux, 1970: 172).

3. "Often described as a royalist uprising, supported by the Church, in fact *chouannerie* started quite simply in protest against suppression of the Breton Assembly; only at a later stage was it infiltrated by royalists" (Mayo, 1974: 32; see also Sérant, 1971: 62).

4. One commentator has written, "Even though a few Félibres at times entertained separatist dreams, the movement as a whole was never of such a nature as to justify the fears that were expressed in the daily press and in the reviews. Barring an extremely small minority, the average Méridional has always considered himself a loyal citizen of France, in no wise inferior to any other Frenchman" (Roche, 1954: 241).

5. In 1892, at a Congress of the Félibrige, Maurras declared, "We are autonomists. We are federalists, and if somewhere in northern France there are people who want to march with us, we hold out our hand to them . . ." (Sérant, 1971: 241).

6. About Ferroul, one historian writes, "For him, this revolt was in continuity with those that had shaken the Southwest since the Cathari, the Albigensian Crusades, the war of the Camisards and the commune of Narbonne. According to him these combats were devoted to the name of freedom of thought, political autonomy and economic survival, and were related to those in Ireland and Catalonia" (Holohan, 1976: 284).

7. Two general histories are Reece (1977) and Sérant (1971). Polemical histories abound; three of these are Caërléon (1971), Lebesque (1970), and Mordrel (1973).

8. The law forbids "whosoever undertakes, in whatever fashion, to undermine the integrity of the national territory or to subtract from the authority of France a part of territory where this authority is exercised" (Law of 23 May 1938).

9. Hobsbawn, however, specifically excludes Corsican banditry from his classification of primitive rebels (Hobsbawm, 1959: 3-4).

10. Kremnitz (1973) shows the same pattern in a more restricted survey of Occitan publications.

11. "It is often far from easy," writes a sympathetic observer, "in reading their texts, to differentiate between the Anarchist-Communist Federation of Occitania, the Occitan Nationalist Party and the People of Occitania. The Occitan Proudhonian tradition is mixed with revolutionary nationalism, with elements borrowed from the feminist movement and the youth movement" (Lafont, 1974: 311).

12. "The FLB-1 (also known as FLB-ARB), whose bombings were spread out between 1966 and 1968, was dismantled by the police in the beginning of 1969. . . . The FLB-2 is a formally recognized political organization, whose statutes were declared at the prefecture of Ille-et-Vilaine in the Autumn of 1969 [this group was subsequently banned by the government]. It was created by extreme left militants (some of whom are members of the Breton Communist Party), but it was not heard of again after its first appearance. The FLB-3 is responsible for eighteen bombings between April 12, 1971 and April 13, 1972. This network was broken up after a recent attack . . ." (*Le Monde*, 28 December 1972). A fourth FLB is known as Breton Liberation Front for Liberation and Socialism (Front de Libération de la Bretagne Pour la Libération Nationale et le Socialisme).

CHAPTER II

1. Parsons's ideas about ethnicity have changed since this original structural-functional formulation. See Parsons, 1975, especially p. 62.

2. This term is so much in vogue nowadays among social scientists on both sides of the Atlantic and of the equator that a note must be made about its varying definitions and interpretations. The empirical contents to which it has been applied include societies of the Third World, the United States, and Europe. In each of these three contexts, it has been applied to

the situation of ethnically distinct people and to that of mere regional underdevelopment. There are thus basically six uses to which the concept of internal colonialism has been put.

CHAPTER III

1. Besides blank and null ballots, a common way of measuring electorally expressed opposition in France is the percentage of abstentions. But these figures are not presented, because their correlations with the independent variable are not substantially different from those of the percentages of blank and null ballots.

2. These are only representative accounts of the events referred to. There are literally hundreds of articles substantiating the ranks assigned to the regions for this measure. For this and the other ethnic regions, only representative articles will be cited.

3. There is more than a logical basis for expecting that rising expectations may explain ethnic conflict in contemporary France. Evidence shows that the improving circumstances of the Flemings in Belgium, a traditionally subordinated minority, led to the explosion of ethnic conflict in Belgium (Mann, 1978: 32).

CHAPTER IV

1. Corsican leaders were not included in the survey because the author originally intended to visit each ethnic region, and it would not have been practical to visit Corsica. For testing the propositions, however, the omission of Corsica will not vitiate their confirmation or rejection.

2. The "other" category is sociologically meaningless, but had to be adopted to make comparisons between the sample and the population. The categories here presented do not include the seventeen students and one housewife who appeared among the respondents, because these are not considered actively employed.

3. Source: INSEE, *Recensement général de la population de 1968; Résultats du sondage au 1/20; Population active.* Paris: Imprimerie Nationale, 1968 p. 74.

References

Allen, R.
1969   *Black Awakening in Capitalist America.* Garden City: Doubleday.
Almaguer, T.
1975   "Class, Race and Chicano Oppression," *Socialist Revolution,* 5, 3.
Almond, G. and G. Powell
1966   *Comparative Politics: A Developmental Approach.* Boston: Little,
        Brown.
Aristotle
1943   *Aristotle's Politics.* New York: Random House.
Atelier Occitan Peire d'Auvernha
(n.d.) *L'Occitanisme: qu'es aquo?*
Aulard, A.
1968   "A Party of Anti-Parisian Republicans," in F. Kafker and J. Laux
        (eds.), *The French Revolution: Conflicting Interpretations.* New
        York: Random House.
Barrera, M., C. Muñoz, and C. Ormelas
1972   "The Barrio as an Internal Colony," in *Politics and People in Urban
        Society: Urban Affairs Annual Reviews,* ed. by H. Hahn, vol. 6.
Barth, F.
1969   *Ethnic Groups and Boundaries.* Boston: Little, Brown.
Bazalgues, G.

1973   "Les Organisations occitanes," *Les Temps Modernes*, 324-326, 140-162.

Beer, W.
1977   "The Social Class of Ethnic Activists in Contemporary France, in M. Esman (ed.), *Ethnic Conflict in the Western World*. Ithaca: Cornell University Press.

Berger, P., B. Berger, and H. Kellner
1974   *The Homeless Mind*. New York: Norton.

Berger, S.
1972   "Bretons, Basques, Scots and Other European Nations," *Journal of Interdisciplinary History*, 3, 167-175.

Bernardo D.
1976   "Catalogne-Nord: le traumatisme de la coupure," *Pluriel-débat*, 7, 5-27.

Bernardo, D. and B. Rieu
1973   "Conflit linguistique et revendications culturelles en Catalogne-Nord," *Les Temps Modernes*, 324-326.

Blauner, R.
1972   *Racial Oppression in America*. New York: Vintage.

Caerleon, R.
1971   *La Révolution bretonne permanente*. Paris.

Calvet, L.
1974   *Linguistique et colonialisme: petit traité de glottophagie*. Paris: Payot.

Carmichael, S. and C. Hamilton
1967   *Black Power: The Politics of Liberation in America*. New York: Random House.

Chatelain, D. and P. Tafani
1976   *Qu'est-ce qui fait courir les autonomistes?* Paris: Stock.

Chevalier, M.
1972   "Le Problème de la personnalité occitane," *Ethnopsychologie*, 4, 371-378.

Cayrol, R.
1969   "Histoire et sociologie d'un parti," in M. Rocard (ed.). *Le PSU et l'avenir socialiste de la France*. Paris: Seuil.

Connor. W.
1972   "Nation-Building or Nation-Destroying?" *World Politics*, 24, 3, 319-355.
1973   "The Politics of Ethnonationalism," *Journal of International Affairs*, 27, 1, 1-21.

1975   "Ethnonationalism in the First World: The Present in Historical Perspective," in M. Esman (ed.), *Ethnic Conflict in the Western World*. Ithaca: Cornell University Press.

Cruse, H.
1968   *Rebellion or Revolution?* New York: Morrow.

DaSilva, M.
1975   "Modernization and Ethnic Conflict: The Case of the Basques," *Comparative Politics*, January.

Davies, J.
1962   "Toward a Theory of Revolution," *American Sociological Review*, February, 5-19.

Dejonghe, E.
1970   "Un Mouvement séparatiste dans le Nord et le Pas-de-Calais sous l'Occupation (1940-1944): le Vlaamse Verbond van Frankrijk," *Revue d'histoire moderne et contemporaine*, 1150-1177.

Desjardins, T.
1977   *La Corse à la dérive*. Paris: Plon.

Deutsch, K.
1953   *Nationalism and Social Communication*. Cambridge: MIT Press.
1961   "Social Mobilization and Political Development," *American Political Science Review*, 55, 3, 493-514.

DeVos, G.
1975   "Ethnic Pluralism: Conflict and Accommodation," in G. DeVos and L. Romanucci-Ross (eds.), *Ethnic Identity: Cultural Continuities and Change*. Palo Alto: Mayfield Press.

Durkheim, E.
1951   *Suicide*. New York: Free Press.

Eisenstadt, S.
1971   "Breakdowns of Modernization," in J. Finkle and R. Gable (eds.), *Political Development and Social Change*, New York: Wiley, 573-591.

Emerson, R.
1962   *From Empire to Nation*. Cambridge: Harvard University Press.

Enloe, C.
1973   *Ethnic Conflict and Political Development*. Boston: Little, Brown.

Erikson, E.
1963   *Childhood and Society*. New York: Norton.

Espieux, H.
1970   *Histoire de l'Occitanie*. Agen: Centre Culturel Occitan.

Fishman, J.
1966 *Language Loyalty in the United States.* The Hague: Mouton.
Fortier, D.
1971 "Breton Nationalism and Modern France: Permanent Revolution," in O. Pi-Sunyer (ed.), *The Limits of Integration: Ethnicity and Nationalism in Modern Europe.* Amherst: University of Massachusetts, Department of Anthropology Monographs, 77-109.
Fougeyrollas, P.
1969 *Pour une France fédérale.* Paris: Denoel.
Francis, E.
1976 *Interethnic Relations: Essays in Comparative Sociology.* New York: Basic Books.
Frères du Monde
1971 "Ferments Révolutionnaires: Bretagne, Corse, Euskadi, Occitanie," Frères du Monde, 70, 1-62.
Frazier, E.
1957 *Black Bourgeoisie.* New York: Free Press.
Galloy, M.
1966 "Euzkadi (Pays Basque)," *Europa Ethnica,* vol. 23, no. 2, 50-57.
Garnier, M. and L. Hazelrigg
1974 "Father-to-Son Occupational Mobility in France: Evidence from the 1960's," *American Journal of Sociology,* vol. 80, 478-502.
Glazer, N. and D. Moynihan
1975 "Introduction," in N. Glazer and D. Moynihan (eds.), *Ethnicity: Theory and Experience.* Cambridge: Harvard University Press.
1963 *Beyond the Melting Pot.* Cambridge: MIT Press.
Gonzales-Casanova. P.
1965 "Internal Colonialism and National Development," *Studies in Comparative International Development,* vol. 1, no. 4, 27-37.
Gorz, A.
1971 "Colonialism at Home and Abroad," *Liberation,* 16, 6, 22-28.
Gramsci, A.
1959 "The Southern Question," in *The Modern Prince and Other Writings.* New York.
Gravier, J.
1972 *Paris et le désert français.* Paris: Flammarion.
Greenwood, D.
1975 "Continuity in Change: Spanish Basque Ethnicity as a Historical Process," in M. Esman (ed.), *Ethnic Conflict in the Western World.* Ithaca: Cornell University Press.

Guin, Y.
1977   *Histoire de Bretagne de 1789 à nos jours.* Paris: Maspero.
Gurr, T.
1970   *Why Men Rebel.* Princeton: Princeton University Press.
Haupt, G., M. Lowy, and C. Weill
1974   *Les Marxistes et la question nationale.* Paris: Maspero.
Havens, E. and W. Flinn
1970   *Internal Colonialism and Structural Change in Colombia.* New York: Praeger.
Hechter, M.
1972   *Internal Colonialism: The Celtic Fringe in British National Development,* 1536-1966. Berkeley: University of California Press.
Heisler, M. (ed.),
1974   *Politics in Europe.* New York: McKay.
Héraud, G.,
1963   *L'Europe des ethnies.* Paris.
1966   *Peuples et langues d'Europe.* Paris.
Hobsbawm, E.
1959   *Primitive Rebels.* New York: Norton.
Hoffet, F.
1951   *Psychanalyse d'Alsace.* Paris: Flammarion.
Holohan, W.
1976   "Le Conflit du Larzac: chronique et essai d'analyse," *Sociologie du travail,* no. 3, 283-301.
Horowitz, I.
1972   *Three Worlds of Development: The Theory and Practice of International Stratification.* New York: Oxford University Press.
Jacob, J.
1978   "Two Types of Ethnic Militancy in France," paper presented at Annual Meeting of the International Studies Association, Washington, D.C.
Jaubert, A., J. Salomon, I. Segal, and N. Weil
1974   *Le Guide de la France des luttes.* Paris: Stock.
Kautsky, J.
1976   "An Essay in the Politics of Underdevelopment," in J. Kautsky (ed.), *Political Change in Underdeveloped Societies.* Huntington: Krieger.
Kremnitz, G.
1973   "La Situation de langue d'oc à travers une enquête sur les mass-media," *Revue des langues romanes,* vol. 80, no. 2, 249-303.

Kuhn, T.
1970 *The Structure of Scientific Revolutions.* Chicago: University of Chicago Press.
Kuligowski, E.
1973 *Le Larzac veut vivre.* Paris: Mauprey.
Lafont, R.
1971 *Clefs pour l'Occitanie.* Paris: Seghers.
1974 *La Revendication occitane.* Paris: Flammarion.
1971 *Le Sud et le nord.* Toulouse: Privat.
Lebesque, M.
1970 *Comment peut-on être breton?* Paris: Seuil.
Legris, M.
1964 "Les Parlers maternels en France," *Le Monde,* 9-18, septembre.
Lenin, V.
1956 *The Development of Capitalism in Russia.* Moscow.
Lipset, S. and R. Bendix
1959 *Social Mobility in Industrial Society.* Berkeley: University of California Press.
Lott, J.
1976 "Migration of a Mentality: The Filipino Community," *Social Casework,* 57, 3, 165-172.
Luke, T.
1978 "Internal Colonialism in the United States: A Preliminary Study of the Mountain West," paper presented at the Caucus for a New Political Science, American Political Science Association.
McDonald, J.
1978 "Europe's Restless Regions: Regional Agitation in the '70's: Brittany, a Case Study," *Focus,* 28, 5 (May-June).
Mann, A.
1978 "Europe's Passionate Separatists," *Atlas,* 25, 10, 30-38.
Mannheim, K.
1962 *Ideology and Utopia.* New York: Harcourt Brace and World.
Marti, C.
1975 *Homme d'Oc.* Paris: Stock.
Marx, K. and F. Engels
1955 *The Communist Manifesto.* New York: Appleton-Century-Crofts.
Maugue, P.
1970 *Le Particularisme alsacien.* Paris: Presses d'Europe.
Mayo, P.
1974 *The Roots of Identity.* London: Allen Lane.

Miller, A.
1971   "Ethnicity and Political Behavior: A Review of Theories and an
       Attempt at a Reformulation," *Western Political Quarterly*, 24, 3,
       483-500.
Miller, A., L. Dolce, and M. Halligan
1977   "The J-Curve Theory and the Black Urban Riots: An Empirical
       Test of the Progressive Relative Deprivation Theory," *American
       Political Science Review*, 71, 964-981.
Mills, C.
1962   "The Problem of Industiral Development," in I. Horowitz (ed.),
       Power, Politics, and People. New York: Ballantine.
Moore, J.
1974   "Colonialism: the Case of the Mexican-Americans," in L. Rainwa-
       ter (ed.), *Inequality and Justice: Social Problems and Public Policy.*
       Chicago: Aldine.
Mordrel, O.
1973   *Breiz Atao: histoire et actualité du nationalisme breton.* Paris:
       Moreau.
Muzellec, R.
1968   "La Consultation pre-référendaire de septembre 1968 en Bretagne
       sur la régionalisation," *Revue du droit publique et science politique*,
       89, 3.
Nairn, T.
1974   "Scotland and Europe," *New Left Review*, no. 83, 57-82.
Nolasco-Armas, M.
1971   "Continuidad y cambio sociocultural en el Norte de México,"
       América Indígena, 31, 2, 323-333.
Novak, M.
1971   *The Rise of the Unmeltable Ethnics.* New York: Macmillan.
Parenti, M.
1967   "Ethnic Politics and the Persistence of Ethnic Identification,"
       American Political Science Review, vol. 61, no. 3, 717-726.
Parsons, T.
1968   *The Social System.* New York: Free Press.
1975   "Some Theoretical Considerations of the Nature and Trends of
       Change of Ethnicity," in N. Glazer and D. Moynihan (eds.), *Eth-
       nicity: Theory and Experience.* Cambridge: Harvard University
       Press.
Patterson, O.
1975   "Context and Choice in Ethnic Allegiance: A Theoretical Frame-

work and Caribbean Case Study," in N. Glazer and D. Moynihan (eds.), *Ethnicity: Theory and Experience.* Cambridge: Harvard University Press.

Pye, L.
1966   *Aspects of Political Development.* Boston: Little, Brown.
Reece, J.
1977   *The Bretons Against France.* Chapel Hill: University of North Carolina Press.
Renan, E.
1910   "The Poetry of the Celtic Races," in *Literary and Philosophical Essays,* Harvard Classics, vol. 32. New York: Collier.
Roche, A.
1954   *Provençal Regionalism.* New York: AMS Press.
Rouanet, M.
1970   *Occitanie 1970: les poètes de la décolonisation.* Honfleur: Oswald.
Sacx, M.
1968   *Bayonne et le Pays Basque.* Bayonne.
Sérant, P.
1965   *La France des minorités.* Paris: Robert Laffont.
1971   *La Bretagne at la France.* Paris: Fayard.
Smith, A.
1971   *Theories of Nationalism.* London: Duckworth.
Stagnara, V.
1976   "Le Sens de la révolution corse," *Les Temps Modernes,* 31, 1670-1686.
Staples, R.
1976   "Race and Colonialism: the Domestic Case," *Black Scholar,* 7, 9.
Tabb, W.
1974   "Marxian Exploitation and Domestic Colonialism: A Reply to Donald J. Harris," *The Review of Black Political Economy,* Summer.
1970   *The Political Economy of the Black Ghetto.* New York: Academic Press.
Stavenhagen, R.
1965   "Classes, Colonialism and Acculturation," *Studies in Comparative International Development,* 1, 6.
Theroux, P.
1978   "A Circuit of Corsica," *Atlantic,* 24, 5, 90-93.
Tilly, C.
1964   *The Vendée.* Cambridge: Harvard University Press.

Tocqueville, A.
1959 *The Old Regime and the French Revolution*. New York: Doubleday.
Tumin, M.
1964 "Ethnic Groups," in J. Gould and W. Kolb (eds.), *A Dictionary of the Social Sciences*. New York: Free Press.
Van den Berghe, P.
1970 *Race and Ethnicity: Essays in Comparative Sociology*. New York: Basic Books.
Vandewalle, E.
1976 "Chronique," in *De Franse Nederlanden/Les Pays-Bas français*. Rekkem: Stichting Ons Erfdeel.
Webb, L.
1971 "Colonialism and Underdevelopment in Vermont," *Liberation*, 16, 6.
Weber, M.
1967 *The Theory of Social and Economic Organization*. New York: Free Press.
1968 *Economy and Society*. New York: Bedminster.
Williams, P.
1970 *French Politicians and Elections: 1951-1969*. Cambridge: Cambridge University Press.

Index